70 VEGETARIAN

EVERY DAY LOW FAT RECIPES

70 vegetarian
every day low fat recipes

70 VEGETARIAN
EVERY DAY LOW FAT RECIPES

Fabulous, fresh and healthy meat-free dishes beautifully illustrated with more than 300 inspirational photographs

Consultant editor: Anne Sheasby

southwater

This edition is published by Southwater, an imprint of
Anness Publishing Ltd, Hermes House, 88–89 Blackfriars Road,
London SE1 8HA; tel. 020 7401 2077; fax 020 7633 9499

www.southwaterbooks.com; www.annesspublishing.com

If you like the images in this book and would like to investigate using them
for publishing, promotions or advertising, please visit our website
www.practicalpictures.com for more information.

UK agent: The Manning Partnership Ltd
  tel. 01225 478444; fax 01225 478440;
  sales@manning-partnership.co.uk
UK distributor: Grantham Book Services Ltd
  tel. 01476 541080; fax 01476 541061; orders@gbs.tbs-ltd.co.uk
North American agent/distributor: National Book Network
  tel. 301 459 3366; fax 301 429 5746; www.nbnbooks.com
Australian agent/distributor: Pan Macmillan Australia
  tel. 1300 135 113; fax 1300 135 103
  customer.service@macmillan.com.au
New Zealand agent/distributor: David Bateman Ltd
  tel. (09) 415 7664; fax (09) 415 8892

Publisher: Joanna Lorenz
Senior Managing Editor: Conor Kilgallon
Editors: James Harrison and Elizabeth Woodland
Recipes: Pepita Aris, Catherine Atkinson, Mary Banks, Alex Barker, Ghillie
  Basan, Judy Bastyra, Angela Boggiano, Jacqueline Clark, Maxine Clark,
  Trish Davies, Roz Denny, Joanna Farrow, Jennie Fleetwood, Brian Glover,
  Nicola Graimes, Carole Handslip, Christine Ingram, Becky Johnson, Lucy
  Knox, Sally Mansfield, Christine McFadden, Jane Milton, Sallie Morris,
  Rena Salaman, Jenni Shapter, Marlena Spieler, Liz Trigg, Jenny White,
  Kate Whiteman, Lucy Whiteman, Jeni Wright.
Home economists: Eliza Baird, Alex Barker, Caroline Barty, Joanna Farrow,
  Annabel Ford, Christine France, Carole Handslip, Kate Jay, Becky
  Johnson, Jill Jones, Bridget Sargeson, Jennie Shapter, Carol Tennant,
  Sunil Vijayakar, Jenny White.
Photographers: Frank Adam, Tim Auty, Martin Brigdale, Louisa Dare,
  Nicki Dowey, Gus Filgate, Ian Garlick, Michelle Garrett, John Heseltine,
  Amanda Heywood, Janine Hosegood, Dave Jordan, Dave King, William
  Lingwood, Thomas Odulate, Craig Roberson, Simon Smith, Sam Stowell.
Designer: Graham Webb, Design Principals
Cover Designer: Nigel Partridge
Production Manager: Steve Lang

Ethical Trading Policy

At Anness Publishing we believe that business should be conducted in
an ethical and ecologically sustainable way, with respect for the
environment and a proper regard to the replacement of the natural
resources we employ.

As a publisher, we use a lot of wood pulp to make high-quality paper
for printing, and that wood commonly comes from spruce trees. We are
therefore currently growing more than 500,000 trees in two Scottish
forest plantations near Aberdeen – Berrymoss (130 hectares/320 acres)
and West Touxhill (125 hectares/305 acres). The forests we manage
contain twice the number of trees employed each year in paper-making
for our books.

Because of this ongoing ecological investment programme, you, as our
customer, can have the pleasure and reassurance of knowing that a tree is
being cultivated on your behalf to naturally replace the materials used to
make the book you are holding.

Our forestry programme is run in accordance with the UK Woodland
Assurance Scheme (UKWAS) and will be certified by the internationally
recognized Forest Stewardship Council (FSC). The FSC is a non-
government organization dedicated to promoting responsible management
of the world's forests. Certification ensures forests are managed in an
environmentally sustainable and socially responsible way. For further
information about this scheme, go to www.annesspublishing.com/trees

© Anness Publishing Ltd 2007

Previously published as part of a larger volume, *Low-Fat,
No-Fat Vegetarian*

Notes

Bracketed terms are intended for American readers.

For all recipes, quantities are given in both metric and imperial measures
and, where appropriate, in standard cups and spoons. Follow one set, but
not a mixture, because they are not interchangeable.

Standard spoon and cup measures are level. 1 tsp = 5ml,
1 tbsp = 15ml, 1 cup = 250ml/8fl oz. Australian standard tablespoons are
20ml. Australian readers should use 3 tsp in place of 1 tbsp for measuring
small quantities of flour, salt, etc.

American pints are 16fl oz/2 cups. American readers should use
20fl oz/2.5 cups in place of 1 pint when measuring liquids.

The nutritional analysis given for each recipe is calculated per portion
(i.e. serving or item), unless otherwise stated. If the recipe gives a range,
such as Serves 4–6, then the nutritional analysis will be for the smaller
portion size, i.e. 6 servings. The nutritional analysis of recipes also excludes
all optional ingredients (where the word 'optional' appears in brackets after
an ingredient), serving suggestions, foods/ingredients 'to serve', croûtons (in
a couple of the soup recipes), garnishes and decorations, as well as
variations and cook's tips. Measurements for sodium do not include salt
added to taste.

Each recipe title in this book is followed by a symbol that indicates
the following:

★ = 5g of fat or less per serving
★★ = 10g of fat or less per serving

We have included cooking temperatures for electric and gas ovens. If you
have a fan-assisted oven, remember that you need to reduce the oven
temperature slightly (usually by around 20°C/40°F) and/or adjust the cooking
times. Please refer to manufacturer's guidelines for more specific
information on adjusting the temperature and time for your oven.

Some of the recipes in this book may contain raw or lightly cooked eggs –
these recipes are not recommended for babies and young children,
pregnant women, the elderly and those convalescing. Medium (US large)
eggs are used unless otherwise stated.

Ideally, home-made low-fat vegetable stock should be used for all relevant
recipes in this book. Alternatively, good quality stock cubes or bouillon
powder can be used.

While every care has been taken in compiling and testing the recipes in this
book, the publisher or any other persons who have been involved in working
on this publication cannot accept responsibility for any errors or omissions,
inadvertent or not, that may be found in the recipes or text, nor for any
problems that may arise as a result of preparing one of these recipes.

CONTENTS

INTRODUCTION

Many people think that vegetarianism is a relatively new trend, but in many countries around the globe, vegetarianism, in one form or another, has been the natural way to eat for many hundreds, if not thousands, of years. Today, there are millions of people who are vegetarians.

Although some vegetarian dishes are high in calories and fat, many can be enjoyed as part of a healthy low-fat eating regime, and with a few basic guidelines, a low-fat vegetarian diet is simple to achieve.

Defining vegetarianism

There are various forms of vegetarianism: you might be a vegan, a lacto-vegetarian, a fruitarian or on a macrobiotic diet. According to the Vegetarian Society, the definition of a vegetarian is "someone living on a diet of grains, pulses, nuts, seeds, vegetables and fruits with or without the use of dairy products and eggs (preferably free-range)".

A vegetarian does not eat any meat, poultry, game, fish, shellfish or crustacea, or meat by-products such as gelatine or animal fats.

A typical vegetarian diet includes a wide range of different food groups such as cereals/grains, pulses, nuts, seeds, fruit and vegetables, as well as dairy or soya products, eggs and vegetable oils and fats. These form the basis of a healthy and nutritious eating regime.

There are several different kinds of vegetarian diets. The most common vegetarians are Lacto-ovo-vegetarians who avoid meat, poultry and fish, etc, but include dairy products and eggs in their diet. Lacto-vegetarians are the same as Lacto-ovo-vegetarians, but they do not eat eggs.

Vegans, on the other hand, follow a much stricter eating regime and do not eat meat, poultry and fish, dairy products, eggs, or any other animal product. Fruitarians eat a diet which consists mainly of raw fruit, grains and nuts. Very few processed or cooked foods are eaten. Finally, some people choose a macrobiotic diet, which is a diet followed for spiritual and philosophical reasons. This specific diet progresses through ten levels, becoming increasingly restrictive.

Above: Onions are known to have excellent culinary and medicinal values.

Although not all levels are vegetarian, each level gradually eliminates animal products until the highest level eventually reaches a brown rice diet.

As long as you eat a wide variety of foods, life never need be dull if you choose to follow a vegetarian diet. By its very nature, a balanced vegetarian diet tends to be naturally low in saturated and total fat, high in dietary fibre and complex carbohydrates, and high in many protective vitamins and minerals. A well-balanced vegetarian diet should provide all the nutrients, vitamins and minerals your body needs.

Through vegetarian cooking, you can mix and match the vibrant colours, textures and flavours of vegetables, fruits, pulses and grains with many other exciting ingredients, and experiment with a wide variety of interesting and unusual foods to create all kinds of delicious and tempting dishes from many parts of the world.

Choosing vegetarian food

Many vegetarian foods available in shops and supermarkets are clearly marked on their packaging as being

Left: Rice is perfect for creating a substantial vegetarian meal.

'suitable for vegetarians'. Some food products also carry the 'V' (vegetarian) symbol and others carry vegetarian symbols familiar to particular countries such as the 'two green leaves' symbol. Some vegetarian foods carry a Vegetarian Society symbol, which indicates that they are approved and meet specific criteria that ensures the foods are absolutely suitable for vegetarians. Other food products, such as cheese, may also include additional useful information, for example advice that the cheese is made using 'non-animal rennet'.

Nutrition and the vegetarian diet

In a vegetarian diet, protein, which is made up of amino acids, is needed for the growth and repair of all body cells. Protein is provided by foods such as eggs, milk, yogurt, cheese and soya bean products, such as tofu and tempeh, all of which contain many of the essential amino acids we need.

Other foods such as beans, peas, lentils, grains, nuts and seeds also provide a valuable source of protein.

Carbohydrates, which divide into simple and complex carbohydrates,

Below: Sweat mushrooms in a little stock rather than butter or use raw in salads. Reconstituted dried mushrooms are excellent for adding intense flavour to sauces, rice and pasta dishes.

Above: Tomatoes on the vine contain vitamin C, folic acid, potassium and lycopene – an antioxidant that can help prevent cancer.

supply the body with energy. Simple carbohydrates tend to be found in sugars and sweet foods, which should only be eaten in moderation. Complex carbohydrates on the other hand are a vital part of a healthy diet and these are provided by foods such as rice, pasta, bread, potatoes and other vegetables, as well as many fruits. Many of these complex carbohydrate foods also provide fibre, vitamins and minerals.

Vitamins and minerals have many vital functions and important roles, such as keeping the nervous system and other tissues healthy, helping to maintain healthy eyes, skin and hair, and to protect against disease. A balanced vegetarian diet should supply many of these, although some vegetarians choose to increase their intake of vitamins and minerals with supplements such as vitamin B12, calcium, iron and zinc.

How to use this book

There are over 70 delicious and easy-to-follow low-fat vegetarian recipes that all the family will enjoy. Our tempting selection of recipes ranges from soups and appetizers, salads and side dishes, to light meals and main course dishes. It also includes a tasty collection of delicious desserts and home-baked cakes.

Each recipe gives a nutritional breakdown, providing at-a-glance calorie and fat contents (including saturated fat content), as well as other key nutrients such as protein, carbohydrate, cholesterol, calcium, fibre and sodium.

As its title suggests, all the recipes in this cookbook are low in fat – the majority containing five grams or less of fat per serving, and some containing less than one gram. The few exceptions are in the chapter entitled 'Main Courses', where the more substantial of the recipes contain ten grams of fat or less per serving.

For ease of reference, throughout the recipe section, all recipes with a single ★ following the recipe name contain five grams of fat or fewer, and those with ★★ contain ten grams of fat or fewer. All the recipes contain even less fat than typical vegetarian recipes yet they are still full of delicious flavour and appeal.

SOUPS AND APPETIZERS

There are many low-fat options when it comes to soups and appetizers — and a tasty soup, served with bread, can be a meal in itself. In this chapter, there is a tempting selection of recipes, from refreshing cold dishes such as Tzatziki or Spiced Yogurt and Cucumber Raita, to warm delights including Curried Parsnip Soup and Roasted Vegetable Lavash Wraps.

TOMATO AND FRESH BASIL SOUP ★

A LIGHT SOUP IDEAL FOR LATE SUMMER, WHEN FRESH PLUM TOMATOES ARE AT THEIR MOST
SUCCULENT, THIS FRESH TOMATO SOUP FLAVOURED WITH BASIL CREATES A TASTY DISH.

SERVES FOUR

INGREDIENTS
  10ml/2 tsp olive oil
  1 onion, finely chopped
  900g/2lb ripe Italian plum tomatoes,
    roughly chopped
  1 garlic clove, roughly chopped
  about 750ml/1¼ pints/3 cups
    vegetable stock
  120ml/4fl oz/½ cup dry white wine
  30ml/2 tbsp sun-dried tomato
    purée (paste)
  30ml/2 tbsp shredded fresh basil,
    plus a few whole leaves to garnish
  30ml/2 tbsp single (light) cream
  salt and ground black pepper

1 Heat the olive oil in a large non-stick
pan over a medium heat. Add the onion
and cook gently for about 5 minutes,
until it is softened but not brown,
stirring frequently.

2 Stir in the chopped tomatoes and
garlic, then add the stock, white wine
and tomato purée, with salt and pepper
to taste. Bring to the boil, then reduce
the heat, half-cover the pan and simmer
gently for 20 minutes, stirring the
mixture occasionally to stop the
tomatoes sticking to the base of the pan.

COOK'S TIP
When buying garlic, choose plump garlic
with tightly packed cloves and dry skin.
Avoid bulbs with soft, shrivelled cloves or
green sprouting shoots.

3 Process the soup with the shredded
basil in a blender or food processor
until smooth, then press the mixture
through a sieve (strainer) into a clean
pan. Discard the contents of the sieve.

4 Add the cream to the soup in the
pan and heat through gently, stirring.
Do not allow the soup to boil. Check the
consistency of the soup and add more
hot stock if necessary, then adjust the
seasoning to taste. Pour into soup bowls
and garnish with whole basil leaves.
Serve immediately.

Energy 97Kcal/409kJ; Protein 2.4g; Carbohydrate 9.6g, of which sugars 9.2g; Fat 3.7g, of which saturates 1.4g; Cholesterol 4mg; Calcium 32mg; Fibre 2.7g; Sodium 42mg.

FARMHOUSE SOUP ★

ROOT VEGETABLES FORM THE BASIS OF THIS DELICIOUS LOW-FAT, CHUNKY, MINESTRONE-STYLE SOUP.
FOR A MORE SUBSTANTIAL MEAL, SERVE IT WITH FRESH CRUSTY BREAD.

SERVES SIX

INGREDIENTS
    15 ml/1 tbsp olive oil
    1 onion, roughly chopped
    3 carrots, cut into large chunks
    175–200g/6–7oz turnips, cut into
      large chunks
    175g/6oz swede (rutabaga), cut into
      large chunks
    400g/14oz can chopped tomatoes
    15ml/1 tbsp tomato purée (paste)
    5ml/1 tsp mixed dried herbs
    5ml/1 tsp dried oregano
    50g/2oz/½ cup dried peppers,
      washed and thinly sliced (optional)
    1.5 litres/2½ pints/6¼ cups
      vegetable stock or water
    50g/2oz/½ cup dried small macaroni
      or conchiglie
    400g/14oz can red kidney beans,
      rinsed and drained
    30ml/2 tbsp chopped fresh
      flat leaf parsley
    salt and ground black pepper
    15ml/1 tbsp freshly grated Parmesan
      cheese, to serve

COOK'S TIP
Dried Italian peppers are piquant and firm with a "meaty" bite, which makes them ideal for adding substance to vegetarian soups.

VARIATIONS
Use 1 red onion in place of standard onion. Use parsnips in place of turnips or swede.

1 Heat the oil in a large non-stick pan, add the onion and cook over a low heat for about 5 minutes, until softened. Add the prepared fresh vegetables, canned tomatoes, tomato purée, dried herbs and dried peppers, if using. Stir in salt and pepper to taste. Pour in the stock or water and bring to the boil. Stir well, then reduce the heat, cover and simmer for 30 minutes, stirring occasionally.

2 Add the pasta and bring to the boil, stirring, then simmer, uncovered, for about 5 minutes or according to the packet instructions, until the pasta is just tender or *al dente*. Stir frequently.

3 Stir in the beans. Heat through for 2–3 minutes, then remove from the heat and stir in the parsley. Adjust the seasoning to taste. Serve hot, sprinkled with a little grated Parmesan.

Energy 161Kcal/678kJ; Protein 7.1g; Carbohydrate 28.2g, of which sugars 12.3g; Fat 3g, of which saturates 0.5g; Cholesterol 0mg; Calcium 100mg; Fibre 7.8g; Sodium 294mg.

ROASTED VEGETABLE SOUP ★

ROASTING THE VEGETABLES, ESPECIALLY THE BUTTERNUT SQUASH, GIVES THIS HEARTY LOW-FAT WINTER SOUP A WONDERFUL DEPTH OF FLAVOUR AND A BEAUTIFUL RICH COLOUR.

SERVES SIX

INGREDIENTS
30ml/2 tbsp olive oil
1 small butternut squash, peeled, seeded and cubed
2 carrots, cut into thick rounds
1 large parsnip, cubed
1 small swede (rutabaga), cubed
2 leeks, washed and thickly sliced
1 onion, quartered
3 bay leaves
4 fresh thyme sprigs, plus extra to garnish
3 fresh rosemary sprigs
1.2 litres/2 pints/5 cups vegetable stock
salt and ground black pepper
sour cream, to serve

1 Preheat the oven to 200°C/400°F/ Gas 6. Pour the oil into a large bowl, add all the prepared vegetables and toss until well coated.

2 Spread out the vegetables in a single layer on one large or two small baking sheets. Tuck the bay leaves, thyme and rosemary sprigs among the vegetables.

COOK'S TIP
To make sure you remove all the dirt and grit from between the leaves of leeks, slit the leeks lengthways, almost to the root end. Hold the leeks under running cold water, fanning out the leaves to wash them well.

3 Roast the vegetables in the oven for about 50 minutes, turning them occasionally to make sure that they brown evenly. Remove from the oven, discard the herbs and transfer the vegetables to a large pan.

4 Pour the stock into the pan and bring to the boil. Reduce the heat, season to taste with salt and pepper, then simmer for 10 minutes. Transfer the soup to a blender or food processor and process until thick and smooth.

5 Return the soup to the rinsed out pan and heat through gently, stirring. Serve in heated bowls, adding a swirl of sour cream to each portion. Garnish with the extra thyme sprigs.

VARIATION
For the butternut squash you might substitute an acorn squash with its sweet flavour but slightly drier texture, or even a pumpkin which is ideal for soups.

Energy 113Kcal/474kJ; Protein 3.1g; Carbohydrate 15.1g, of which sugars 10.4g; Fat 4.9g, of which saturates 0.8g; Cholesterol 0mg; Calcium 105mg; Fibre 6g; Sodium 18mg.

WILD MUSHROOM SOUP ★

DRIED PORCINI MUSHROOMS — THE KING OF MUSHROOMS IN ITALIAN COOKING — ARE PRICY BUT HAVE AN INTENSE FLAVOUR SO ONLY A SMALL QUANTITY IS NEEDED FOR THIS DELICIOUS LIGHT SOUP.

SERVES FOUR

INGREDIENTS

25g/1oz/½ cup dried porcini
  mushrooms
10ml/2 tsp olive oil
2 leeks, thinly sliced
2 shallots, roughly chopped
1 garlic clove, roughly chopped
225g/8oz/3 cups fresh wild
  mushrooms
about 1.2 litres/2 pints/5 cups
  vegetable stock
2.5ml/½ tsp dried thyme
30ml/2 tbsp single (light) cream
salt and ground black pepper
fresh thyme sprigs, to garnish

1 Put the dried porcini mushrooms in a bowl, add 250ml/8fl oz/1 cup warm water and leave to soak for 20–30 minutes. Lift the mushrooms out of the liquid and squeeze over the bowl to remove as much of the soaking liquid as possible. Strain all the liquid and reserve to use later. Finely chop the porcini and set aside.

2 Heat the olive oil in a large, non-stick pan. Add the leeks, shallots and garlic and cook gently for about 5 minutes, stirring the mixture frequently, until softened but not coloured.

COOK'S TIP
Store dried herbs, such as dried thyme, in airtight glass containers, and keep them in a cool, dark place.

3 Chop or slice the fresh mushrooms and add to the pan. Stir over a medium heat for a few minutes until they begin to soften. Pour in the stock and bring to the boil. Add the chopped porcini, reserved soaking liquid, dried thyme and salt and pepper to taste. Reduce the heat, half-cover the pan and simmer gently for 30 minutes, stirring occasionally.

4 Pour about three-quarters of the soup into a blender or food processor and process until smooth. Return to the soup left in the pan, stir in the cream and heat through gently, stirring. Check the consistency and add more hot stock if the soup is too thick. Adjust the seasoning to taste. Serve hot in soup bowls, garnished with fresh thyme sprigs.

Energy 62Kcal/257kJ; Protein 3.1g; Carbohydrate 4.2g, of which sugars 3.1g; Fat 3.8g, of which saturates 1.3g; Cholesterol 4mg; Calcium 36mg; Fibre 2.9g; Sodium 8mg.

TUSCAN BEAN SOUP ★

CAVOLO NERO IS A VERY DARK GREEN CABBAGE WITH A NUTTY FLAVOUR. IT'S AVAILABLE IN MOST LARGE SUPERMARKETS, BUT IF YOU CAN'T GET IT, TRY SAVOY CABBAGE. SERVE WITH CIABATTA BREAD.

SERVES FOUR

INGREDIENTS
  2 x 400g/14oz cans chopped
    tomatoes with herbs
  250g/9oz cavolo nero leaves
  400g/14oz can cannellini beans
  10ml/2 tsp extra virgin olive oil
  salt and ground black pepper

1 Pour the tomatoes into a large pan and add a can of cold water. Season to taste with salt and pepper. Bring to the boil, then reduce the heat to a simmer.

2 Roughly shred the cabbage leaves and add them to the pan. Half-cover the pan and simmer gently for about 15 minutes, or until the cabbage is tender.

3 Drain and rinse the cannellini beans, then add them to the pan and heat through for a few minutes until hot. Check and adjust the seasoning to taste, then ladle the soup into bowls. Drizzle each portion with a little olive oil and serve.

Energy 164Kcal/696kJ; Protein 9.2g; Carbohydrate 27.1g, of which sugars 12.9g; Fat 2.8g, of which saturates 0.5g; Cholesterol 0mg; Calcium 116mg; Fibre 9.5g; Sodium 413mg.

PASTA, BEAN AND VEGETABLE SOUP ★★

THIS TASTY SOUP IS A SPECIALITY FROM THE CALABRIAN REGION OF ITALY. THE COMBINATION OF PULSES, PASTA AND VEGETABLES CREATES A FILLING LOW-FAT SOUP.

SERVES SIX

INGREDIENTS
75g/3oz/scant ½ cup brown lentils
15g/½oz/¼ cup dried mushrooms
15ml/1 tbsp olive oil
1 carrot, diced
1 celery stick, diced
1 onion, finely chopped
1 garlic clove, finely chopped
a little chopped fresh flat leaf parsley
a good pinch of dried crushed
  red chillies (optional)
1.5 litres/2½ pints/6¼ cups
  vegetable stock
150g/5oz/scant 1 cup each canned
  red kidney beans, cannellini beans
  and chickpeas, rinsed and drained
115g/4oz/1 cup dried small pasta
  shapes, such as rigatoni or penne
salt and ground black pepper
chopped fresh flat parsley to garnish
30ml/2 tbsp freshly grated Pecorino
  cheese, to serve

1 Put the lentils in a medium pan, add 475ml/16fl oz/2 cups water and bring to the boil over a high heat. Reduce the heat to a gentle simmer and cook, for 15–20 minutes, or until just tender, stirring occasionally. Meanwhile, soak the dried mushrooms in 175ml/6fl oz/ ¾ cup warm water for 15–20 minutes.

2 Put the lentils into a sieve (strainer) to drain, then rinse under the cold tap. Drain the soaked mushrooms and reserve the soaking liquid. Finely chop the mushrooms and set aside.

3 Heat the oil in a large, non-stick pan and add the carrot, celery, onion, garlic, parsley and chillies, if using. Cook over a low heat for 5–7 minutes, stirring occasionally. Add the stock, then the mushrooms and their soaking liquid.

4 Bring to the boil, then add the beans, chickpeas and lentils. Season to taste with salt and pepper. Cover and simmer gently for 20 minutes.

5 Add the pasta and bring the soup back to the boil, stirring. Reduce the heat, then simmer, for 7–8 minutes, or according to the packet instructions, until the pasta is tender or *al dente*, stirring frequently. Adjust the seasoning to taste, then serve hot, sprinkled with chopped parsley and grated Pecorino.

VARIATIONS
Use 3–4 shallots in place of onion. Use freshly grated Parmesan cheese in place of Pecorino.

Energy 205Kcal/869kJ; Protein 10.7g; Carbohydrate 36.4g, of which sugars 5.2g; Fat 2.9g, of which saturates 0.4g; Cholesterol 0mg; Calcium 72mg; Fibre 6.3g; Sodium 304mg.

CREAMY CAULIFLOWER SOUP ★

THIS SOUP IS LIGHT IN FLAVOUR AND FAT YET SATISFYING ENOUGH FOR A LUNCHTIME SNACK.
YOU CAN TRY GREEN CAULIFLOWER FOR A COLOURFUL CHANGE.

3 Add the cauliflower, dill, lemon juice, mustard powder and caraway seeds and simmer for a further 20 minutes.

4 Process the soup in a blender or food processor until smooth, then return the soup to the rinsed-out pan and stir in the milk. Reheat gently, stirring. Season to taste with salt and pepper and serve garnished with shredded spring onions.

COOK'S TIP

For a special treat, use single cream in place of some or all of the milk, but remember this will add both calories and fat to this recipe.

SERVES SIX

INGREDIENTS
 15ml/1 tbsp olive oil
 2 large onions, finely chopped
 1 garlic clove, crushed
 3 large floury potatoes, finely diced
 3 celery sticks, finely diced
 1.75 litres/3 pints/7½ cups
   vegetable stock
 2 carrots, finely diced
 1 medium cauliflower, chopped
 15ml/1 tbsp chopped fresh dill
 15ml/1 tbsp lemon juice
 5ml/1 tsp mustard powder
 1.5ml/¼ tsp caraway seeds
 300ml/½ pint/1¼ cups
   semi-skimmed (low-fat) milk
 salt and ground black pepper
 shredded spring onions (scallions),
   to garnish

1 Heat the oil in a large, non-stick pan, add the onions and garlic and cook for a few minutes until they soften. Add the potatoes, celery and stock and bring to the boil, then reduce the heat and simmer for 10 minutes, stirring occasionally.

2 Add the carrots and simmer for a further 10 minutes, stirring occasionally.

Energy 169Kcal/711kJ; Protein 7.4g; Carbohydrate 27.7g, of which sugars 10.8g; Fat 4g, of which saturates 1.1g; Cholesterol 3mg; Calcium 111mg; Fibre 4g; Sodium 55mg.

CURRIED PARSNIP SOUP ★

THE MILD SWEETNESS OF PARSNIPS WITH SWEET MANGO CHUTNEY IS GIVEN AN EXCITING LIFT WITH A BLEND OF SPICES IN THIS DELICIOUS, SIMPLE, LIGHT VEGETARIAN SOUP.

SERVES FOUR

INGREDIENTS

   10ml/2 tsp olive oil
   1 onion, chopped
   1 garlic clove, crushed
   1 small green chilli, seeded and
    finely chopped
   15ml/1 tbsp grated fresh root ginger
   5 large parsnips, diced
   5ml/1 tsp cumin seeds
   5ml/1 tsp ground coriander
   2.5ml/½ tsp ground turmeric
   30ml/2 tbsp sweet mango chutney
   1.2 litres/2 pints/5 cups water
   juice of 1 lime
   salt and ground black pepper
   60ml/4 tbsp low-fat natural (plain)
    yogurt and sweet mango chutney,
    to serve
   chopped fresh coriander (cilantro),
    to garnish (optional)
For the sesame naan croûtons (to serve)
   15ml/1 tbsp olive oil
   1 large naan bread, cut into
    small dice
   15ml/1 tbsp sesame seeds

1 Heat the oil in a large, non-stick pan and add the onion, garlic, chilli and ginger. Cook for 4–5 minutes, until the onion has softened, stirring occasionally. Add the parsnips and cook for 2–3 minutes. Sprinkle in the cumin seeds, ground coriander and turmeric, and cook for 1 minute, stirring constantly.

2 Add the chutney and the water. Season well and bring to the boil. Reduce the heat and simmer for 15 minutes, until the parsnips are soft.

3 Cool the soup slightly, then process it in a blender or food processor until smooth, then return it to the rinsed-out pan. Stir in the lime juice.

4 To make the naan croûtons, heat the oil in a large, non-stick frying pan and cook the diced naan bread for 3–4 minutes, until golden all over, stirring. Remove the pan from the heat and drain off any excess oil. Add the sesame seeds and return to the heat for 30 seconds, until the seeds are pale golden.

5 Ladle the soup into bowls. Spoon a little yogurt into each portion, then top with a little mango chutney and some of the sesame naan croûton mixture. Garnish with chopped coriander, if you like.

Energy 58Kcal/244kJ; Protein 3.3g; Carbohydrate 3.8g, of which sugars 0.3g; Fat 3.6g, of which saturates 0.9g; Cholesterol 95mg; Calcium 16mg; Fibre 0g; Sodium 304mg.

FRESH BROAD BEAN AND POTATO SOUP ★

THIS LIGHT SOUP USES FRESH BROAD BEANS MIXED WITH CORIANDER TO GIVE AN INVIGORATING FLAVOUR TO A HEARTY DISH. FRESH BEANS NEED TO BE SHELLED FIRST.

SERVES FOUR

INGREDIENTS

  10ml/2 tsp olive oil
  2 onions, chopped
  3 large floury potatoes
  450g/1lb fresh shelled broad
    (fava) beans
  1.75 litres/3 pints/7½ cups
    vegetable stock
  a bunch of fresh coriander (cilantro),
    roughly chopped
  150ml/¼ pint/⅔ cup semi-skimmed
    (low-fat) milk
  salt and ground black pepper
  single (light) cream, to garnish

1 Heat the oil in a large, non-stick pan and cook the onions for 5 minutes until soft, stirring. Add the potatoes, most of the beans (reserving a few for the garnish) and the stock, and bring to the boil. Simmer for 5 minutes, then add the coriander and simmer for a further 10 minutes.

2 Process the soup in batches in a blender or food processor, then return to the rinsed out pan.

3 Stir in the milk and seasoning. Heat gently until almost boiling, stirring. Serve garnished with coriander, beans and cream.

Energy 263Kcal/1113kJ; Protein 13.9g; Carbohydrate 47g, of which sugars 10.8g; Fat 3.5g, of which saturates 0.9g; Cholesterol 2mg; Calcium 142mg; Fibre 10.2g; Sodium 45mg.

CREAMY CORN AND POTATO CHOWDER ★

THIS CHUNKY LOW-FAT SOUP IS RICH WITH THE SWEET TASTE OF CORN. IT'S EXCELLENT SERVED WITH
THICK CRUSTY BREAD AND TOPPED WITH A LITTLE MELTED, REDUCED-FAT CHEDDAR CHEESE.

SERVES SIX

INGREDIENTS
  1 onion, chopped
  1 garlic clove, crushed
  1 medium baking potato, chopped
  2 celery sticks, sliced
  1 small green (bell) pepper, seeded,
    halved and sliced
  15ml/1 tbsp sunflower oil
  600ml/1 pint/2½ cups vegetable
    stock or water
  300ml/½ pint/1¼ cups
    semi-skimmed (low-fat) milk
  200g/7oz can flageolet or small
    cannellini beans
  300g/11oz can corn kernels
  a good pinch of dried sage
  salt and ground black pepper
  reduced-fat Cheddar cheese, grated,
    to serve (optional)

1 Put the fresh vegetables into a large, non-stick pan with the oil.

2 Heat the pan until the vegetables are sizzling, then reduce the heat to low. Cover and cook gently for about 10 minutes, shaking the pan occasionally.

3 Pour in the stock or water, season to taste with salt and pepper and bring to the boil. Reduce the heat, cover again and simmer gently for about 15 minutes, or until the vegetables are tender.

4 Add the milk, the beans and corn kernels (including their liquids) and the sage. Simmer, uncovered, for 5 minutes. Adjust the seasoning and serve hot, sprinkled with cheese, if you like.

Energy 181Kcal/766kJ; Protein 6.8g; Carbohydrate 32.1g, of which sugars 12.7g; Fat 3.8g, of which saturates 0.9g; Cholesterol 3mg; Calcium 106mg; Fibre 4.2g; Sodium 298mg.

SPICED YOGURT AND CUCUMBER RAITA ★

THESE SLIGHTLY SOUR, YOGURT-BASED DISHES HAVE A COOLING EFFECT ON THE PALATE WHEN EATEN WITH SPICY, LOW-FAT INDIAN FOODS. THEY CREATE A TASTY LOW-FAT SNACK.

SERVES FOUR

INGREDIENTS
FOR THE SPICED YOGURT
450ml/¾ pint/scant 2 cups low-fat natural (plain) yogurt
2.5ml/½ tsp freshly ground fennel seeds
2.5ml/½ tsp granulated sugar
25ml/5 tsp vegetable oil
1 dried red chilli
1.5ml/¼ tsp mustard seeds
1.5ml/¼ tsp cumin seeds
4–6 curry leaves
a pinch each of asafoetida and ground turmeric
salt

1 In a bowl, mix together the yogurt, fennel and sugar, and add salt to taste. Chill in the refrigerator.

2 Heat the oil in a non-stick pan and fry the remaining ingredients. When the chilli turns dark, pour the oil and spices over the yogurt and mix. Chill before serving.

SERVES SIX

INGREDIENTS
FOR THE CUCUMBER RAITA
½ cucumber
1 fresh green chilli, seeded and chopped
300ml/½ pint/1¼ cups low-fat natural (plain) yogurt
1.5ml/¼ tsp salt
1.5ml/¼ tsp ground cumin

1 Dice the cucumber finely and place in a large mixing bowl. Add the chilli.

2 Beat the yogurt with a fork until smooth, then stir into the cucumber and chilli mixture.

3 Stir in the salt and cumin. Cover the bowl with clear film (plastic wrap) and chill before serving.

VARIATION
Instead of using cucumber, try two skinned, seeded and chopped tomatoes and 15ml/1 tbsp chopped fresh coriander (cilantro).

Yogurt: Energy 110kcal/460kJ; Protein 6.3g; Carbohydrate 10.4g, of which sugars 9.1g; Fat 5.4g, of which saturates 1.1g; Cholesterol 1mg; Calcium 221mg; Fibre 0g; Sodium 95mg.
Raita: Energy 31kcal/131kJ; Protein 2.8g; Carbohydrate 4.2g, of which sugars 4g; Fat 0.6g, of which saturates 0.3g; Cholesterol 1mg; Calcium 104mg; Fibre 0.2g; Sodium 141mg.

TZATZIKI ★

A GREEK CUCUMBER SALAD DRESSED WITH YOGURT, MINT AND GARLIC, TZATZIKI MAKES A REFRESHING LOW-FAT VEGETARIAN STARTER. IT'S BEST SERVED WITH FRESH VEGETABLE CRUDITÉS.

SERVES FOUR

INGREDIENTS

1 cucumber
5ml/1 tsp salt
45ml/3 tbsp finely chopped fresh
  mint, plus a few sprigs
  to garnish
1 garlic clove, crushed
5ml/1 tsp caster (superfine) sugar
200ml/7fl oz/scant 1 cup
  reduced fat Greek (US strained
  plain) yogurt

1 Peel the cucumber. Reserve a little of the cucumber to use as a garnish if you wish and cut the rest in half lengthways. Remove the seeds with a teaspoon and discard. Slice the cucumber thinly and combine with the salt in a bowl. Leave for approximately 15–20 minutes. Salt will soften the cucumber and draw out any bitter juices.

2 Combine the mint, garlic, sugar and yogurt in a separate bowl, reserving a few sprigs of mint as decoration.

3 Rinse the cucumber in a sieve (strainer) under cold running water to flush away the salt. Drain well and combine with the yogurt. Serve cold.

COOK'S TIPS
• If you want to prepare Tzatziki in a hurry, then leave out the method for salting the cucumber at the end of Step 1. The cucumber will have a more crunchy texture, and will be slightly less sweet.
• Wash fresh herbs, such as mint, before use. Simply wash the herbs by shaking them quickly under cold running water. Drain well and dry on kitchen paper, then chop or use as required.

Energy 41Kcal/170kJ; Protein 3.2g; Carbohydrate 6.1g, of which sugars 5.9g; Fat 0.6g, of which saturates 0.3g; Cholesterol 1mg; Calcium 110mg; Fibre 0.5g; Sodium 535mg.

MUSHROOM CAVIAR ★

THE NAME CAVIAR REFERS TO THE DARK COLOUR AND TEXTURE OF THIS LOW-FAT VEGETARIAN DISH OF CHOPPED MUSHROOMS. SERVE WITH TOASTED RYE BREAD RUBBED WITH CUT GARLIC CLOVES.

SERVES FOUR

INGREDIENTS

15ml/1 tbsp olive or vegetable oil
450g/1lb mushrooms, coarsely
  chopped
5–10 shallots, chopped
4 garlic cloves, chopped
salt
boiled egg, spring onions and herbs,
  chopped, to garnish (optional)

VARIATION

For a rich wild mushroom caviar, soak 10–15g/¼–½oz dried porcini in about 120ml/4fl oz/½ cup water for about 30 minutes. Add the porcini and their soaking liquid to the browned mushrooms in Step 2. Continue as in the recipe. Serve with wedges of lemon.

1 Heat the oil in a large, non-stick pan, add the mushrooms, shallots and garlic, and cook until browned, stirring occasionally. Season with salt, then continue cooking until the mushrooms give up their liquor.

2 Continue cooking until the liquor has evaporated and the mushrooms are brown and dry, stirring frequently.

3 Put the mixture in a blender or food processor and process briefly until a chunky paste is formed. Spoon the mushroom caviar into dishes and serve.

Energy 68Kcal/283kJ; Protein 3.3g; Carbohydrate 6.4g, of which sugars 3.8g; Fat 3.5g, of which saturates 0.5g; Cholesterol 0mg; Calcium 24mg; Fibre 2.4g; Sodium 8mg.

VEGETABLE PANCAKES WITH TOMATO SALSA ★

THESE DELICIOUS SPINACH AND EGG PANCAKES MAKE A GREAT LOW-FAT VEGETARIAN APPETIZERS OR SNACK, IDEAL SERVED WITH A TASTY TOMATO SALSA.

MAKES TEN

INGREDIENTS
   225g/8oz fresh spinach leaves
   1 small leek
   a few sprigs of fresh coriander
      (cilantro) or fresh parsley
   3 large (US extra large) eggs
   50g/2oz/½ cup plain (all-purpose)
      flour, sifted
   15ml/1 tbsp sunflower oil
   25g/1oz/⅓ cup freshly grated
      Parmesan cheese
   salt, ground black pepper and freshly
      grated nutmeg
For the salsa
   2 tomatoes, skinned and chopped
   ¼ fresh red chilli, finely chopped
   2 pieces sun-dried tomato in oil,
      drained and chopped
   1 small red onion, finely chopped
   1 garlic clove, crushed
   60ml/4 tbsp tomato juice
   30ml/2 tbsp sherry
   2.5ml/½ tsp soft light brown sugar

1 Prepare the tomato salsa: place all the ingredients in a bowl and toss together to combine. Cover and leave to stand in a cool place for 2–3 hours.

2 To make the pancakes, finely shred or chop the spinach, leek and coriander or parsley. If you prefer, chop them in a food processor, but do not overprocess. Place the chopped vegetables in a bowl and beat in the eggs and seasoning. Blend in the flour and 30–45ml/ 2–3 tbsp water, then leave to stand for 20 minutes.

3 To cook the pancakes, drop spoonfuls of the batter into a lightly oiled frying pan and cook until golden underneath. Using a fish slice or metal spatula, turn the pancakes over and cook briefly on the other side.

4 Carefully lift the pancakes out of the pan, drain on kitchen paper and keep warm while you cook the remaining mixture in the same way. Sprinkle the pancakes with grated Parmesan cheese and serve with the salsa.

VARIATION
Use 3–4 spring onions (scallions) in place of leek.

COOK'S TIP
Try to find sun-ripened tomatoes for the salsa, as these have the best and sweetest flavour and are much superior to those ripened under glass.

Energy 70Kcal/294kJ; Protein 4.5g; Carbohydrate 6.2g, of which sugars 2.1g; Fat 2.9g, of which saturates 1.1g; Cholesterol 60mg; Calcium 91mg; Fibre 1.3g; Sodium 96mg.

ROASTED VEGETABLE LAVASH WRAPS ★

MIDDLE-EASTERN FLATBREADS ARE PERFECT FOR SNACK-TIME LOW-FAT WRAPS. TEAR OFF SUITABLY SIZED PIECES TO WRAP, FOLD OR ROLL UP FRAGRANT ROASTED VEGETABLES.

SERVES SIX

INGREDIENTS
    3 courgettes (zucchini), trimmed and
      sliced lengthways
    1 large fennel bulb, cut into wedges
    450g/1lb butternut squash, seeded
      and cut into 2cm/¾in chunks
    12 shallots
    2 red (bell) peppers, seeded and
      cut lengthways into thick slices
    4 plum tomatoes, halved and seeded
    30ml/2 tbsp extra virgin olive oil
    2 garlic cloves, crushed
    5ml/1 tsp balsamic vinegar
    salt and ground black pepper
To serve
    lavash or other flat bread
    a little fresh or good quality bottled pesto
    chopped fresh mint
    low-fat Greek (US strained plain) yogurt
    a little feta cheese, diced

1 Preheat the oven to 220°C/425°F/ Gas 7. Place the courgettes, fennel, butternut squash, shallots, red peppers and tomatoes in a large bowl. Add the olive oil, garlic and balsamic vinegar and toss until all the ingredients are thoroughly coated in the mixture. Set aside for about 10 minutes to allow the flavours to mingle.

2 Using a slotted spoon, lift just the tomatoes and butternut squash out of the mixture and set them aside on a plate. Use the spoon to transfer all the remaining vegetables to a large roasting pan. Brush with half the oil and vinegar mixture remaining in the bowl, season with salt and pepper and roast in the oven for 25 minutes.

3 Remove the pan from the oven and turn the vegetables over. Brush with the remaining oil and vinegar mixture, add the squash and tomatoes and roast for a further 20–25 minutes, or until all the vegetables are tender and have begun to char around the edges.

4 Put the bread on the table, with the pesto, mint, yogurt and feta cheese in separate bowls. Spoon the roasted vegetables on to a large platter and invite everyone to tuck in.

VARIATION
Use vine-ripened tomatoes in place of plum tomatoes.

Energy 109Kcal/453kJ; Protein 4.1g; Carbohydrate 13g, of which sugars 11.5g; Fat 4.8g, of which saturates 0.8g; Cholesterol 0mg; Calcium 72mg; Fibre 4.6g; Sodium 14mg.

ROASTED RED PEPPER AND TOMATO SALAD ★

THIS IS ONE OF THOSE LOVELY RECIPES THAT BRINGS TOGETHER PERFECTLY THE COLOURS, FLAVOURS AND TEXTURES OF SOUTHERN ITALIAN FOOD. EAT THIS LOW-FAT STARTER OR SNACK AT ROOM TEMPERATURE.

SERVES FOUR

INGREDIENTS

3 red (bell) peppers
6 large plum tomatoes, halved
2.5ml/½ tsp dried red chilli flakes
1 red onion, finely sliced
3 garlic cloves, thinly chopped
finely grated rind and juice
  of 1 lemon
45ml/3 tbsp chopped fresh flat
  leaf parsley
15ml/1 tbsp extra virgin olive oil
salt
black and green olives and extra
  chopped flat leaf parsley, to garnish

COOK'S TIP
These peppers will keep for several weeks if the peeled pepper pieces are placed in a jar of olive oil, with a tight-fitting lid. Store in the refrigerator.

1 Preheat the oven to 220°C/425°F/ Gas 7. Place the peppers on a baking sheet and roast for 10 minutes until the skins are slightly blackened. Add the tomatoes and bake for 5 minutes more.

2 Place the peppers in a plastic bag. Close the top loosely, trapping in the steam, and then set them aside, with the tomatoes, until they are cool.

3 Skin and seed the peppers. Chop the peppers and tomatoes roughly and place them both in a mixing bowl.

4 Add the chilli flakes, onion, garlic and lemon rind and juice. Sprinkle over the parsley. Mix well, then transfer to a serving dish. Season with salt, drizzle over the olive oil and sprinkle the olives and extra parsley over the top. Serve.

Energy 96Kcal/400kJ; Protein 2.7g; Carbohydrate 13.4g, of which sugars 12.6g; Fat 3.8g, of which saturates 0.7g; Cholesterol 0mg; Calcium 46mg; Fibre 4.1g; Sodium 22mg.

SALADS AND SIDE DISHES

Vegetarian salads and side dishes offer
plenty of scope for imaginative
combinations of vegetables, fruits, herbs
and spices. The collection presented here
includes Avocado and Pink Grapefruit
Salad, Fresh Asparagus with Lemon Sauce,
Braised Leeks with Carrots, and Fennel,
Potato and Garlic Mash.

ASPARAGUS, TOMATO AND ORANGE SALAD ★

THIS LIGHT SALAD ORIGINATES FROM SPAIN, WHERE COOKS SIMPLY RELY ON THE WONDERFUL TASTE OF A GOOD-QUALITY OLIVE OIL. USE EXTRA VIRGIN OLIVE OIL TO BRING OUT THE BEST FLAVOUR.

SERVES SIX

INGREDIENTS

   350g/12oz asparagus, trimmed and
     cut into 5cm/2in pieces
   2 large oranges
   2 well-flavoured tomatoes, cut
     into eighths
   50g/2oz cos or romaine lettuce
     leaves, shredded
   30ml/2 tbsp extra virgin olive oil
   2.5ml/½ tsp sherry vinegar
   salt and ground black pepper

VARIATIONS
• Little Gem (Bibb) lettuce can be used
in place of cos lettuce.
• Grapefruit segments also work well in
this salad. Use 1 ruby grapefruit instead
of the oranges.

1 Cook the asparagus in a pan of salted boiling water for 3–4 minutes, or until just tender. Drain and refresh under cold water. Set aside.

2 Grate the rind from half an orange and reserve. Peel both the oranges and cut the flesh into segments. Squeeze out the juice from the membrane and reserve it.

3 Put the asparagus, orange segments, tomatoes and lettuce into a salad bowl. Make the dressing by whisking together the oil and vinegar and adding 15ml/ 1 tbsp of the reserved orange juice and 5ml/1 tsp of the grated rind. Season to taste with salt and pepper. Just before serving, pour the dressing over the salad and toss gently to coat.

Energy 73Kcal/304kJ; Protein 2.6g; Carbohydrate 6.6g, of which sugars 6.5g; Fat 4.2g, of which saturates 0.6g; Cholesterol 0mg; Calcium 44mg; Fibre 2.3g; Sodium 6mg.

ROCKET, PEAR AND PARMESAN SALAD ★

FOR A SOPHISTICATED SALAD TRY THIS SIMPLE ITALIAN-STYLE COMBINATION OF FRESH, RIPE PEARS, TASTY PARMESAN AND AROMATIC LEAVES OF ROCKET. SERVE WITH FRESH ITALIAN BREAD OR CRISPBREADS.

SERVES FOUR

INGREDIENTS
   3 ripe pears, such as Williams
      or Packhams
   10ml/2 tsp lemon juice
   15ml/1 tbsp hazelnut or walnut oil
   115g/4oz rocket (arugula) leaves
   25g/1oz/⅓ cup fresh
      Parmesan cheese
   ground black pepper

1 Peel and core the pears and slice them thickly. Place in a bowl and toss gently with the lemon juice to keep the flesh white.

2 In a bowl, combine the nut oil with the pears. Add the rocket leaves and toss gently to mix.

COOK'S TIP
You can grow your own rocket (arugula) from early spring to late summer. You can also use watercress instead of rocket.

3 Divide the salad among four small plates and top each portion with shavings of Parmesan cheese. Season with pepper and serve immediately.

Energy 100Kcal/416kJ; Protein 3.1g; Carbohydrate 11.7g, of which sugars 11.7g; Fat 4.7g, of which saturates 1.3g; Cholesterol 5mg; Calcium 121mg; Fibre 3.1g; Sodium 98mg.

AVOCADO AND PINK GRAPEFRUIT SALAD ★

ON ITS OWN OR SERVED AS A LIGHT VEGETARIAN SIDE DISH OR FIRST COURSE, THIS BITTER-SWEET SALAD CAN BE PARTIALLY PREPARED IN ADVANCE, BUT DON'T LET THE AVOCADO DISCOLOUR.

2 Put the sugar and water in a small pan and heat gently until the sugar has dissolved. Add the shreds of orange rind, increase the heat and boil steadily for 5 minutes, or until the rind is tender. Using two forks, remove the orange rind from the syrup and spread it out on a wire rack to dry. Reserve the cooking syrup to add to the dressing, if you like.

3 Wash and dry the lettuce or other salad leaves and tear or chop them into bitesize pieces. Using a sharp knife, remove the pith from the oranges and the pith and peel from the grapefruit. Hold the citrus fruits over a bowl and cut out each segment leaving the membrane behind. Squeeze the remaining juice from the membrane into the bowl.

4 Put the French dressing into a screw-top jar with the garlic and mustard, if using. Add the reserved syrup, if using, put the lid on and shake well to combine. Adjust the seasoning to taste. Arrange the salad ingredients on plates with the cubed avocado. Spoon over the dressing and sprinkle with the caramelized peel. Serve.

SERVES EIGHT

INGREDIENTS
  mixed red and green lettuce or other
    salad leaves
  2 sweet pink grapefruit
  1 large or 2 small avocados, peeled,
    stoned (pitted) and cubed
  120ml/4fl oz/½ cup low-fat French
    dressing
  1 garlic clove, crushed
  5ml/1 tsp Dijon mustard (optional)
  salt and ground black pepper
For the caramelized peel
  4 oranges
  50g/2oz/¼ cup caster
    (superfine) sugar
  60ml/4 tbsp cold water

1 To make the caramelized peel, using a vegetable peeler, carefully remove the rind from the oranges in thin strips and reserve the fruit. Scrape away the white pith from the underside of the rind with a small, sharp knife, and cut the rind into fine shreds.

COOK'S TIP
To stop avocado flesh discolouring, brush with a citrus fruit – lemon, orange or lime – juice if you are not planning to eat your avocado at once.

Energy 43Kcal/180kJ; Protein 0.7g; Carbohydrate 4.7g, of which sugars 4.4g; Fat 2.5g, of which saturates 0.5g; Cholesterol 0mg; Calcium 14mg; Fibre 1.1g; Sodium 227mg.

ITALIAN THREE-COLOUR SALAD ★

THIS VIBRANT ITALIAN DISH, KNOWN AS INSALATA TRICOLORE, *CREATES AN APPETIZING AND COLOURFUL FIRST COURSE OR SNACK. USE PLUM OR VINE-RIPENED TOMATOES FOR THE BEST FLAVOUR.*

SERVES SIX

INGREDIENTS

   1 small red onion, thinly sliced
   6 large well-flavoured tomatoes
   50g/2oz/1 small bunch rocket (arugula)
     or watercress, roughly chopped
   115g/4oz reduced-fat mozzarella
     cheese, thinly sliced or grated
   20ml/4 tsp extra virgin olive oil
   30ml/2 tbsp pine nuts (optional)
   salt and ground black pepper

1 Soak the onion slices in a bowl of cold water for 30 minutes, then drain and pat dry. Set aside.

2 Prepare the tomatoes for skinning by slashing them with a sharp knife and dipping them briefly in boiling water.

VARIATIONS
Instead of the fresh rocket or watercress, use chopped fresh basil, which goes particularly well with the flavour of ripe tomatoes. To reduce the fat content even further, omit the oil and sprinkle the salad with a fat-free vinaigrette dressing.

3 Peel off and discard the skins, then thinly slice each tomato.

4 Arrange half the tomato slices on a large platter, or divide them among six small plates, if you prefer.

5 Layer with half the chopped rocket or watercress and half the onion slices, seasoning well with salt and pepper. Add half the mozzarella cheese, sprinkling over a little more seasoning as you go.

6 Repeat with the remaining tomato and onion slices, salad leaves and mozzarella cheese.

7 Season well to finish, then sprinkle the oil over the salad. Scatter the pine nuts over the top, if using. Cover the salad and chill for at least 2 hours before serving. Serve with fresh crusty bread.

Energy 66Kcal/277kJ; Protein 2.9g; Carbohydrate 4g, of which sugars 3.8g; Fat 4.4g, of which saturates 1.8g; Cholesterol 6mg; Calcium 60mg; Fibre 1.3g; Sodium 61mg.

BAKED SWEET POTATO SALAD ★

THIS DELICIOUS SALAD HAS A TRULY TROPICAL TASTE AND IS IDEAL SERVED WITH LOW-FAT VEGETARIAN ASIAN OR CARIBBEAN DISHES. IT ALSO MAKES A TASTY SNACK.

SERVES SIX

INGREDIENTS
1kg/2¼lb sweet potatoes
For the dressing
45ml/3 tbsp chopped fresh
   coriander (cilantro)
juice of 1 lime
150ml/¼ pint/⅔ cup low-fat natural
   (plain) yogurt
For the salad
1 red (bell) pepper, seeded and
   finely chopped
3 celery sticks, finely chopped
¼ red onion, finely chopped
1 fresh red chilli, seeded and
   finely chopped
salt and ground black pepper
fresh coriander (cilantro) leaves,
   to garnish

1 Preheat the oven to 200°C/400°F/ Gas 6. Wash and pierce the potatoes all over, then bake them in the oven for 40 minutes or until tender.

COOK'S TIP
Wash sweet potatoes well and cook them whole because most of the nutrients are next to the skin.

2 Meanwhile, mix the dressing ingredients together in a bowl. Season to taste with salt and pepper. Chill while you prepare the remaining ingredients.

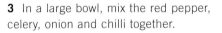

3 In a large bowl, mix the red pepper, celery, onion and chilli together.

4 Remove the potatoes from the oven and when cool enough to handle, peel them. Cut the potatoes into cubes and add them to the bowl. Drizzle the dressing over the salad and toss carefully. Adjust the seasoning to taste and serve, garnished with coriander leaves.

Energy 173Kcal/739kJ; Protein 3.8g; Carbohydrate 40.2g, of which sugars 13.9g; Fat 0.9g, of which saturates 0.3g; Cholesterol 0mg; Calcium 101mg; Fibre 4.8g; Sodium 101mg.

SIMPLE MIXED VEGETABLE RICE SALAD ★

IN THIS QUICK AND EASY SIDE DISH, RICE AND A SELECTION OF CHOPPED SALAD VEGETABLES ARE SERVED IN A TASTY LOW-FAT DRESSING TO CREATE A PRETTY AND SATISFYING VEGETARIAN SALAD.

SERVES SIX

INGREDIENTS
  275g/10oz/scant 1½ cups long
    grain rice
  1 bunch spring onions (scallions),
    thinly sliced
  1 green (bell) pepper, seeded and
    finely chopped
  1 yellow (bell) pepper, seeded and
    finely chopped
  225g/8oz tomatoes, skinned, seeded
    and chopped
  30ml/2 tbsp chopped fresh flat leaf
    parsley or coriander (cilantro)
  salt and ground black pepper
For the dressing
  90ml/6 tbsp low-fat vinaigrette
  5ml/1 tsp strong Dijon mustard
    (optional)

1 Cook the rice in a large pan of lightly salted boiling water for 10–12 minutes, or until tender but still *al dente*. Be careful not to overcook it.

2 Drain the rice well in a sieve (strainer), rinse thoroughly under cold running water and drain again. Leave the rice to cool completely.

3 Place the rice in a large serving bowl. Add the spring onions, peppers, tomatoes and parsley or coriander.

4 If using mustard in the dressing, place the ingredients in a screw-top jar, put the lid on and shake vigorously until well mixed. Stir the dressing into the rice, then adjust the seasoning, to taste.

Energy 199Kcal/834kJ; Protein 4.6g; Carbohydrate 43.5g, of which sugars 6.6g; Fat 0.7g, of which saturates 0.1g; Cholesterol 0mg; Calcium 23mg; Fibre 1.6g; Sodium 232mg.

FRESH ASPARAGUS WITH LEMON SAUCE ★

FRESH ASPARAGUS CAN BE LIGHTLY STEAMED OR BOILED, AND IS A TASTY, LOW-FAT NUTRITIOUS SIDE DISH. THE SAUCE HAS A LIGHT, FRESH TASTE AND BRINGS OUT THE BEST IN ASPARAGUS.

2 Drain the asparagus well (reserving 200ml/7fl oz/scant 1 cup of the cooking liquid) and arrange the spears attractively in a serving dish. Set aside.

3 Blend the cornflour with the cooled, reserved cooking liquid and place in a small pan. Bring to the boil, stirring constantly with a wooden spoon, then cook over a gentle heat until the sauce thickens slightly. Stir in the sugar, then remove the pan from the heat and allow to cool slightly.

4 Beat the egg yolks thoroughly with the lemon juice and stir gradually into the cooled sauce. Cook the sauce over a very low heat until it thickens, stirring constantly. Be careful not to overheat the sauce or it may curdle. Once the sauce has thickened, remove the pan from the heat and continue stirring for 1 minute. Season to taste with salt or sugar, if necessary. Allow the sauce to cool slightly.

5 Stir the cooled lemon sauce, then pour a little over the cooked asparagus. Cover and chill for at least 2 hours, before serving the chilled asparagus accompanied by the remaining lemon sauce.

SERVES FOUR

INGREDIENTS
  675g/1½lb asparagus, tough ends
    removed, and tied in a bundle
  15ml/1 tbsp cornflour (cornstarch)
  10ml/2 tsp unrefined granulated sugar
  2 egg yolks
  juice of 1½ lemons
  salt

COOK'S TIP
Use tiny or baby asparagus spears for an elegant appetizer for a special dinner party.

1 Cook the bundle of asparagus in a pan of salted boiling water for 7–10 minutes.

COOK'S TIP
When buying asparagus, choose plump, even stalks with tightly-budded, compact heads.

Energy 96Kcal/399kJ; Protein 6.4g; Carbohydrate 9.5g, of which sugars 5.8g; Fat 3.8g, of which saturates 1g; Cholesterol 101mg; Calcium 59mg; Fibre 2.9g; Sodium 8mg.

COURGETTES <u>IN</u> TOMATO SAUCE ★

THIS RICHLY FLAVOURED MEDITERRANEAN DISH CAN BE SERVED HOT OR COLD AS A LIGHT SIDE DISH. CUT THE COURGETTES INTO FAIRLY THICK SLICES, SO THAT THEY STAY SLIGHTLY CRUNCHY.

SERVES FOUR

INGREDIENTS

- 15ml/1 tbsp extra virgin olive oil or sunflower oil
- 1 onion, chopped
- 1 garlic clove, chopped
- 4 courgettes (zucchini), thickly sliced
- 400g/14oz can tomatoes
- 2 tomatoes, skinned, seeded and chopped
- 5ml/1 tsp vegetable bouillon powder
- 15ml/1 tbsp tomato purée (paste)
- salt and ground black pepper

1 Heat the oil in a heavy, non-stick pan, add the onion and garlic and cook for 5 minutes, until the onion is softened, stirring occasionally. Add the courgettes and cook for a further 5 minutes, stirring occasionally.

2 Add the canned and fresh tomatoes, bouillon powder and tomato purée. Stir well, then simmer for 10–15 minutes or until the sauce is thickened and the courgettes are just tender. Season to taste with salt and pepper and serve.

Energy 89Kcal/370kJ; Protein 4.3g; Carbohydrate 9.2g, of which sugars 8.6g; Fat 4.1g, of which saturates 0.7g; Cholesterol 0mg; Calcium 54mg; Fibre 3.2g; Sodium 235mg.

BRAISED LEEKS WITH CARROTS ★

SWEET CARROTS AND LEEKS GO WELL TOGETHER ESPECIALLY WHEN TOPPED WITH A LITTLE CHOPPED MINT OR CHERVIL. THIS IS A GOOD LOW-FAT ACCOMPANIMENT TO A VEGETARIAN NUT ROAST SUNDAY LUNCH.

SERVES SIX

INGREDIENTS
  25g/1oz/2 tbsp butter or
    30ml/2 tbsp olive oil
  675g/1½lb carrots, thickly sliced
  2 fresh bay leaves
  75ml/5 tbsp water
  675g/1½lb leeks, cut into 5cm/
    2in lengths
  120ml/4fl oz/½ cup white wine
  30ml/2 tbsp chopped fresh mint
    or chervil
  salt and ground black pepper

1 Heat 15g/½oz/1 tbsp of the butter or 15ml/1 tbsp of the oil in a non-stick pan and cook the carrots gently for 4–5 minutes.

2 Add the bay leaves, water and seasoning to the pan. Bring to the boil, cover loosely and cook for 10–15 minutes, until the carrots are tender. Uncover, then boil the cooking juices until they have all evaporated, leaving the carrots moist and glazed.

VARIATIONS
• Use chopped fresh tarragon in place of mint or chervil.
• Use shallots, sliced, in place of leeks.

3 Meanwhile, heat the remaining 15g/ ½oz/1 tbsp butter or 15ml/1 tbsp oil in a deep, non-stick frying pan or wide pan that will take the sliced leeks in a single layer. Add the leeks and cook them very gently in the melted butter or oil over a medium to low heat for 4–5 minutes, without allowing them to turn brown.

4 Add the wine, half the chopped herb and seasoning. Heat until simmering, then cover and cook gently for 5–8 minutes, until the leeks are tender, but not collapsed.

5 Uncover the leeks and turn them in the buttery juices. Increase the heat slightly, then boil the liquid rapidly until reduced to a few tablespoons.

6 Add the carrots to the leeks, toss together to mix, then reheat them gently. Adjust the seasoning to taste, if necessary. Transfer to a warmed serving dish and serve sprinkled with the remaining chopped herbs.

Energy 108Kcal/451kJ; Protein 2.5g; Carbohydrate 12.3g, of which sugars 11g; Fat 4.3g, of which saturates 2.4g; Cholesterol 9mg; Calcium 58mg; Fibre 5.2g; Sodium 57mg.

VEGETABLE FLORETS POLONAISE ★

SIMPLE STEAMED VEGETABLES BECOME SOMETHING SPECIAL WITH THIS PRETTY EGG TOPPING. THEY MAKE A PERFECT LOW-FAT DINNER PARTY SIDE DISH OR ARE GREAT WITH A WEEKDAY VEGETARIAN SUPPER.

SERVES SIX

INGREDIENTS

500g/1¼lb mixed vegetables, such as cauliflower, broccoli, romanesco and calabrese
25g/1oz/2 tbsp butter or 30ml/1 tbsp extra virgin olive oil
finely grated rind of ½ lemon
1 large garlic clove, crushed
25g/1oz/½ cup fresh breadcrumbs, lightly baked or grilled (broiled) until crisp
1 large (US extra large) egg, hard-boiled
salt and ground black pepper

VARIATION

Use wholemeal (whole-wheat) breadcrumbs instead of the white crumbs. They will give a nuttier flavour and crunchier texture.

1 Trim the vegetables and break into equal size florets. Place the florets in a steamer over a pan of boiling water and steam for 5–7 minutes, until just tender.

2 Toss the steamed vegetables in butter or oil, then transfer them to a serving dish.

3 While the vegetables are cooking, mix together the lemon rind, garlic, baked or grilled (broiled) breadcrumbs and seasoning. Finely chop the egg and mix together with the breadcrumb mixture. Sprinkle the chopped egg combination over the cooked vegetables and serve immediately.

Energy 71Kcal/297kJ; Protein 5.2g; Carbohydrate 4.7g, of which sugars 1.4g; Fat 3.6g, of which saturates 0.7g; Cholesterol 32mg; Calcium 57mg; Fibre 2.3g; Sodium 50mg.

ROASTED POTATOES, PEPPERS AND SHALLOTS ★

THESE POTATOES SOAK UP BOTH THE TASTE AND WONDERFUL AROMAS OF THE SHALLOTS AND ROSEMARY, TO CREATE A DELICIOUS LOW-FAT DISH — JUST WAIT TILL YOU OPEN THE OVEN DOOR.

SERVES FOUR

INGREDIENTS

> 500g/1¼lb waxy potatoes
> 12 shallots
> 2 yellow (bell) peppers
> 15ml/1 tbsp olive oil
> 2 fresh rosemary sprigs
> salt and ground black pepper
> crushed peppercorns, to garnish

1 Preheat the oven to 200°C/400°F/ Gas 6. Par-boil the potatoes in their skins in a pan of salted boiling water for 5 minutes. Drain and when they are cool, peel them and halve lengthways.

VARIATION
Use red (bell) peppers in place of yellow peppers.

2 Peel the shallots, allowing them to fall into their natural segments. Cut each pepper lengthways into eight strips, discarding the seeds and pith.

3 Oil a shallow ovenproof dish with a little olive oil. Arrange the potatoes and peppers in alternating rows and stud with the shallots.

4 Cut the rosemary sprigs into 5cm/2in lengths and tuck among the vegetables. Season the vegetables generously with salt and pepper, add the olive oil, then roast, uncovered, for 30–40 minutes, until all the vegetables are tender. Turn the vegetables occasionally to cook and brown evenly. Serve hot or at room temperature, with crushed peppercorns.

Energy 176Kcal/742kJ; Protein 4.2g; Carbohydrate 33.6g, of which sugars 12.6g; Fat 3.7g, of which saturates 0.6g; Cholesterol 0mg; Calcium 40mg; Fibre 4.1g; Sodium 20mg.

FENNEL, POTATO AND GARLIC MASH ★

*THIS FLAVOURSOME MASH OF POTATO, FENNEL AND GARLIC CREATES A DELICIOUS LIGHT
ACCOMPANIMENT TO VEGETARIAN SAUSAGES, BURGERS OR CUTLETS.*

SERVES SIX

INGREDIENTS
    1 head of garlic, separated
     into cloves
    800g/1¾lb potatoes, cut into chunks
    2 large fennel bulbs
    25g/1oz/2 tbsp butter or 30ml/
     2 tbsp extra virgin olive oil
    120–150ml/4–5fl oz/½–⅔ cup
     semi-skimmed (low-fat) milk or
     single (light) cream
    freshly grated nutmeg
    salt and ground black pepper

1 If using a food mill to mash the potato, leave the garlic unpeeled, otherwise peel it. Cook the garlic with the potatoes in a pan of salted boiling water for 20 minutes.

2 Meanwhile, trim and roughly chop the fennel, reserving any feathery tops. Chop the tops and set aside. Heat 15g/½oz/1 tbsp of the butter or 15ml/1 tbsp of the oil in a heavy non-stick pan. Add the fennel, cover and cook gently for 20–30 minutes, until soft but not browned.

3 Drain and mash the potatoes and garlic. Purée the fennel in a food mill or food processor and beat it into the potato with the remaining butter or oil.

COOK'S TIP
A food mill is good for mashing potatoes as it ensures a smooth texture. Never mash potatoes in a blender or food processor as this releases the starch, giving a result that resembles wallpaper paste.

4 Warm the milk in a pan and beat sufficient into the potato and fennel to make a creamy, light mixture. Season to taste with salt, pepper and nutmeg.

5 Reheat gently, then beat in any chopped fennel tops. Transfer to a warmed dish and serve immediately.

VARIATIONS
• For a stronger garlic flavour, use 30–45ml/2–3 tbsp roasted garlic purée (paste).
• To give a stronger fennel flavour, cook 2.5–5ml/½–1 tsp ground fennel seeds with the fennel.
• For an even healthier mash, substitute hot vegetable stock for some or all of the milk.

Energy 144Kcal/608kJ; Protein 4g; Carbohydrate 24.4g, of which sugars 4.6g; Fat 4.1g, of which saturates 2.3g; Cholesterol 10mg; Calcium 60mg; Fibre 4g; Sodium 61mg.

SAFFRON RICE <u>WITH</u> ONION <u>AND</u> CARDAMOM ★

THIS DELIGHTFULLY FRAGRANT AND ATTRACTIVE, LIGHT PILAFF IS WONDERFUL ACCOMPANIMENT TO SERVE WITH BOTH INDIAN AND MIDDLE-EASTERN VEGETARIAN DISHES.

SERVES FOUR

INGREDIENTS

350g/12oz/generous 1½ cups
  basmati rice
a good pinch of saffron threads
  (about 15 threads)
15g/½oz/1 tbsp butter
1 onion, finely chopped
6 green cardamom pods,
  lightly crushed
5ml/1 tsp salt
2–3 fresh bay leaves
600ml/1 pint/2½ cups vegetable
  stock or water

1 Put the rice into a sieve (strainer) and rinse it well under cold running water. Put it into a bowl, add cold water to cover and set aside to soak for 30–40 minutes. Drain in the sieve.

2 Toast the saffron threads in a dry pan over a low heat for 1–2 minutes, then place in a small bowl and add 30ml/ 2 tbsp warm water. Leave to soak for 10–15 minutes.

3 Melt the butter in a heavy, non-stick pan, add the onion and cardamom pods and cook very gently for 8–10 minutes, until soft and buttery yellow.

4 Add the drained rice and stir to coat the grains. Add the salt and bay leaves, followed by the stock and saffron with its liquid. Bring to the boil, stir, then reduce the heat to very low and cover tightly. Cook for 10–12 minutes, until the rice has absorbed all the liquid.

5 Lay a clean, folded dish towel over the pan under the lid and press on the lid to wedge it firmly in place. Leave to stand for 10–15 minutes.

6 Fluff up the grains of rice with a fork. Turn it into a warmed serving dish and serve immediately.

COOK'S TIP
After boiling, when all the liquid has been absorbed, basmati rice is set aside to finish cooking in its own heat and become tender. Wedging a folded dish towel under the pan lid ensures the heat is not lost and the steam is absorbed.

Energy 348Kcal/1452kJ; Protein 6.7g; Carbohydrate 71g, of which sugars 0.9g; Fat 3.6g, of which saturates 2g; Cholesterol 8mg; Calcium 21mg; Fibre 0.2g; Sodium 515mg.

STIR-FRIED BROCCOLI <u>AND</u> SESAME SEEDS ★

PURPLE SPROUTING BROCCOLI HAS BEEN USED FOR THIS TASTY, LIGHT RECIPE, BUT AN ORDINARY VARIETY OF BROCCOLI, SUCH AS CALABRESE, WORKS JUST AS WELL. SOY SAUCE IS ESSENTIAL.

SERVES TWO

INGREDIENTS
225g/8oz purple sprouting broccoli
5ml/1 tsp olive oil
10ml/2 tsp soy sauce
10ml/2 tsp toasted sesame seeds
salt and ground black pepper

COOK'S TIP
Sesame seeds are widely used in cooking, and they add a delicious, nutty flavour to many dishes. Sesame seeds are available in three different colours – beige (unhulled), black (found in Asian stores) and pearly white. Sesame seeds are also ground into two types of oil – a light, almost tasteless oil for frying, and a dark toasted oil used in small quantities as a flavouring.

1 Using a sharp knife, cut off and discard any thick stems from the broccoli and cut the broccoli into long, thin florets.

2 Heat the oil in a non-stick wok or large, non-stick frying pan and add the broccoli. Stir-fry for 3–4 minutes, or until tender, adding a splash of water if the pan becomes too dry.

3 Add the soy sauce to the broccoli, then season to taste with salt and pepper. Add the sesame seeds and toss to combine, then serve immediately.

VARIATIONS
Use poppy, sunflower or pumpkin seeds in place of sesame seeds.
Use sesame oil in place of olive oil.

Energy 68Kcal/282kJ; Protein 5.6g; Carbohydrate 2.5g, of which sugars 2.1g; Fat 4g, of which saturates 0.7g; Cholesterol 0mg; Calcium 81mg; Fibre 3.1g; Sodium 366mg.

LIGHT MEALS

*A light meal makes an ideal low-fat lunch
— which is good news as there are plenty of
recipes to choose from. The selection is as
varied as it is plentiful: try classic and
innovative recipes such as Potato Gnocchi,
Vegetable Tofu Burgers or Ratatouille, all
of which combine full flavours with a
light touch on the calories and fat.*

POTATO GNOCCHI ★

GNOCCHI ARE LITTLE ITALIAN DUMPLINGS MADE EITHER WITH MASHED POTATO AND FLOUR, AS HERE, OR WITH SEMOLINA. THEY SHOULD BE LIGHT IN TEXTURE, AND MUST NOT BE OVERWORKED WHILE BEING MADE. GNOCCHI ARE IDEAL SERVED WITH GRILLED OR ROASTED MEDITERRANEAN VEGETABLES.

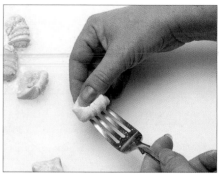

5 Hold an ordinary table fork with long tines sideways, leaning on the board. One by one, press and roll the gnocchi lightly along the tines of the fork towards the points, making ridges on one side and a depression from your thumb on the other.

6 Bring a large pan of water to a fast boil. Add salt and drop in about half the gnocchi.

7 When they rise to the surface, after 3–4 minutes, the gnocchi are done. Scoop them out, allow to drain and place in a warmed serving bowl. Dot with butter. Keep warm while the remaining gnocchi are boiling.

8 As soon as they are cooked, toss the drained gnocchi with the butter and chopped parsley, sprinkle with a little grated Parmesan, if using, and serve.

SERVES SIX

INGREDIENTS

1kg/2¼lb waxy potatoes, scrubbed
250–300g/9–11oz/2¼–2½ cups
  plain (all-purpose) flour
1 egg
pinch of freshly grated nutmeg
small bunch of parsley sprigs, chopped
25g/1oz/2 tbsp butter
salt
a little grated fresh Parmesan cheese,
  to serve (optional)

VARIATION

• Green gnocchi are made in exactly the same way as potato gnocchi, with the addition of fresh or frozen spinach. Use 675g/1½lb fresh spinach, or 400g/14oz frozen leaf spinach. Mix with the potato and the flour in Step 2.

• Almost any pasta sauce is suitable for serving with gnocchi; they are particularly good with a fresh tomato sauce, or simply drizzled with a little olive oil. Gnocchi can also be served in clear low-fat soup.

1 Place the unpeeled potatoes in a large pan of salted water. Bring to the boil and cook until the potatoes are tender but not falling apart. Drain. Peel as soon as possible, while the potatoes are still hot.

2 On a work surface, spread out a layer of flour. Mash the hot potatoes with a food mill, dropping them on to the flour. Sprinkle with about half of the remaining flour. Mix the flour very lightly into the potatoes.

3 Break the egg into the mixture, add the nutmeg and knead lightly, drawing in more flour as necessary. When the dough is light to the touch and no longer moist or sticky, it is ready to be rolled. Do not overwork or the gnocchi will be heavy.

4 Divide the dough into four portions. On a lightly floured board, form each portion into a roll about 2cm/¾in in diameter, taking care not to overhandle the dough. Cut the rolls crossways into pieces about 2cm/¾in long.

Energy 296Kcal/1254kJ; Protein 7.8g; Carbohydrate 59.2g, of which sugars 2.8g; Fat 4.7g, of which saturates 2.3g; Cholesterol 39mg; Calcium 74mg; Fibre 3g; Sodium 52mg.

BAKED POTATOES AND THREE FILLINGS ★

POTATOES BAKED IN THEIR SKINS UNTIL THEY ARE CRISP ON THE OUTSIDE AND FLUFFY IN THE MIDDLE MAKE AN EXCELLENT AND NOURISHING LIGHT MEAL ON THEIR OWN. FOR AN EVEN BETTER TREAT, ADD ONE OF THESE DELICIOUS AND EASY LOW-FAT TOPPINGS. EACH TOPPING IS ENOUGH FOR FOUR BAKED POTATOES.

SERVES FOUR

INGREDIENTS
4 medium baking potatoes
10ml/2 tsp olive oil
salt
filling of your choice (see below)

1 Preheat the oven to 200°C/400°F/ Gas 6. Score the potatoes with a cross and lightly rub all over with the olive oil.

2 Place on a baking sheet and cook in the oven for 45 minutes to 1 hour, until a knife inserted into the centres indicates they are cooked. Or, cook the potatoes in the microwave according to your manufacturer's instructions.

3 Cut the potatoes open along the score lines and push up the flesh. Season and fill with your chosen filling.

RED BEAN CHILLIES
425g/15oz can red kidney beans, rinsed and drained
200g/7oz/scant 1 cup low-fat cottage cheese
30ml/2 tbsp mild chilli sauce
5ml/1 tsp ground cumin

1 Heat the beans in a pan on the hob (stovetop) or in a microwave until hot. Stir in the cottage cheese, chilli sauce and cumin.

2 Fill the baked potatoes with the bean mixture and top with a little chilli sauce.

STIR-FRIED VEGETABLES
10ml/2 tsp sunflower oil
2 leeks, thinly sliced
2 carrots, cut into sticks
1 courgette (zucchini), thinly sliced
115g/4oz baby corn, halved
115g/4oz/1½ cup button (white) mushrooms, sliced
45ml/3 tbsp soy sauce
30ml/2 tbsp dry sherry or vermouth
10ml/2 tsp sesame oil
sesame seeds, to garnish

1 Heat the oil in a non-stick wok or large frying pan until really hot. Add the veg and stir-fry for about 2 minutes, then add the mushrooms and stir-fry for a further minute.

2 Mix the soy sauce, sherry and sesame oil and pour on.

3 Heat through until just bubbling, then scatter over the sesame seeds. Serve.

HERBY-CHEESE AND CORN
425g/15oz can creamed corn
50g/2oz half-fat hard cheese, grated
5ml/1 tsp mixed dried herbs
fresh parsley sprigs, to garnish

1 Gently heat the corn in a pan with the cheese and mixed herbs until well blended and hot.

2 Use to fill the potatoes and garnish with fresh parsley sprigs.

COOK'S TIP
Choose potatoes which are evenly sized and have undamaged skins, and scrub them thoroughly. If they are done before you are ready to serve them, take them out of the oven and wrap them up in a warmed cloth until they are needed.

Red Bean Chillies: Energy 270Kcal/1147kJ; Protein 14.9g; Carbohydrate 48.2g, of which sugars 8.8g; Fat 3.3g, of which saturates 1g; Cholesterol 3mg; Calcium 125mg; Fibre 6.3g; Sodium 563mg.
Stir-fried Vegetables: Energy 225Kcal/950kJ; Protein 7.4g; Carbohydrate 39g, of which sugars 8.3g; Fat 4.5g, of which saturates 0.8g; Cholesterol 0mg; Calcium 55mg; Fibre 5.5g; Sodium 1161mg.
Cheese and Corn: Energy 304Kcal/1290kJ; Protein 10.6g; Carbohydrate 60.5g, of which sugars 12.8g; Fat 3.9g, of which saturates 1.7g; Cholesterol 5mg; Calcium 121mg; Fibre 3.5g; Sodium 393mg.

HUSK-GRILLED CORN <u>ON THE</u> COB ★

KEEPING THE HUSK ON THE CORN PROTECTS THE KERNELS AND ENCLOSES THE JUICES, SO THE FLAVOURS ARE CONTAINED. IF YOU CAN'T GET FRESH HUSKS USE A DOUBLE LAYER OF FOIL.

2 Place the butter in a bowl and add the chillies, lemon juice and parsley. Season to taste with salt and pepper and mix well.

3 Peel back the husks from each cob without tearing them. Remove the silk. Smear a little of the chilli butter over each cob. Pull the husks back over the cobs, ensuring that the butter is well hidden. Put any remaining butter in a small pot, smooth the top and chill to use later. Place the cobs in a bowl of cold water and leave in a cool place for 1–3 hours; longer if that suits your work plan better.

4 Prepare the barbecue, if using, or heat the grill (broiler) to its highest setting. Remove the corn cobs from the water and wrap in pairs in foil. Once the flames have died down, position a lightly oiled grill rack over the coals to heat. When the coals are medium-hot, or have a moderate coating of ash, cook the corn for 15–20 minutes. Remove the foil and cook them for a further 5 minutes, turning them often to char the husks a little. Serve hot, with any remaining butter.

SERVES EIGHT

INGREDIENTS

   1–2 dried chipotle chillies
   40g/1½oz/3 tbsp butter, softened
   2.5ml/½ tsp lemon juice
   15–30ml/1–2 tbsp chopped fresh
    flat leaf parsley
   8 corn on the cob, with husks intact
   salt and ground black pepper

1 Heat a heavy frying pan. Add the dried chillies and roast them by stirring them continuously for 1 minute without letting them scorch.

   Put the chillies in a bowl with almost boiling water to cover. Use a saucer to keep them submerged, and leave them to rehydrate for up to 1 hour. Drain, remove the seeds and chop the chillies finely.

Energy 114Kcal/477kJ; Protein 1.8g; Carbohydrate 16.7g, of which sugars 6g; Fat 4.9g, of which saturates 2.7g; Cholesterol 11mg; Calcium 3mg; Fibre 0.9g; Sodium 199mg.

VEGETABLE TOFU BURGERS ★

THESE SOFT GOLDEN PATTIES ARE STUFFED FULL OF DELICIOUS VEGETABLES. THEY ARE QUICK AND EASY TO MAKE AND ARE LOW IN FAT TOO. SERVE IN SESAME SEED BAPS WITH SALAD AND KETCHUP.

MAKES EIGHT BURGERS

INGREDIENTS
4 potatoes, diced
250g/9oz frozen mixed vegetables,
  such as corn, green beans, (bell)
  peppers
30ml/2 tbsp vegetable oil
2 leeks, coarsely chopped
1 garlic clove, crushed
250g/9oz firm tofu, drained and
  crumbled
30ml/2 tbsp soy sauce
15ml/1 tbsp tomato purée (paste)
115g/4oz/2 cups fresh breadcrumbs
a small bunch of fresh coriander
  (cilantro) or parsley (optional)
salt and ground black pepper

COOK'S TIP
To preserve their vitamins, cook the potatoes whole for 20 minutes, then peel.

1 Cook the potatoes in a pan of salted boiling water for 10–12 minutes, until tender, then drain. Meanwhile, cook the frozen vegetables in a separate pan of salted boiling water for 5 minutes, or until tender, then drain well.

2 Heat 10ml/2 tsp of the oil in a large, non-stick frying pan. Add the leeks and garlic and cook over a low heat for about 5 minutes, until softened and golden, stirring occasionally.

3 Mash the potatoes, then add the vegetables and all the other ingredients except the oil but including the cooked leeks and garlic. Season to taste with salt and pepper, mix together well, then divide the mixture into eight equal size mounds.

4 Squash and shape each mound into a burger. Heat another 10ml/2 tsp oil in the frying pan. Cook four burgers at a time over a gentle heat for 4–5 minutes on each side, until golden brown and warmed through. Repeat with the other four burgers, using the remaining oil. Keep the first batch warm in a low oven. Serve hot.

Energy 167Kcal/704kJ; Protein 6.7g; Carbohydrate 25.7g, of which sugars 3.3g; Fat 4.9g, of which saturates 0.6g; Cholesterol 0mg; Calcium 201mg; Fibre 2.4g; Sodium 391mg.

CHEESE-TOPPED ROAST BABY VEGETABLES ★

THIS IS A SIMPLE WAY OF SERVING TENDER BABY VEGETABLES. ROASTING THEM REALLY BRINGS OUT THEIR SWEET FLAVOUR, AND THE ADDITION OF CHEESE MAKES THIS A TASTY, LIGHT MEAL.

SERVES SIX

INGREDIENTS

   1kg/2¼lb mixed baby vegetables,
     such as aubergines (eggplants),
     onions or shallots, courgettes
     (zucchini), corn cobs and
     mushrooms
   1 red (bell) pepper, seeded and cut
     into large pieces
   1–2 garlic cloves, finely chopped
   15ml/1 tbsp olive oil
   30ml/2 tbsp chopped mixed
     fresh herbs
   225g/8oz cherry tomatoes
   115g/4oz/1 cup coarsely grated
     half-fat mozzarella cheese
   salt and ground black pepper
   black olives, to serve (optional)

1 Preheat the oven to 220°C/425°F/Gas 7. Cut the mixed baby vegetables in half lengthways.

2 Place them and the pepper pieces in an ovenproof dish with the garlic. Add salt and pepper. Drizzle with oil and toss the vegetables to lightly coat them in the oil.

3 Bake in the oven for 20 minutes, or until the vegetables are tinged brown at the edges.

4 Remove from the oven and stir in the chopped herbs. Sprinkle the cherry tomatoes over the surface and top with the grated mozzarella cheese. Return to the oven and bake for a further 5–10 minutes, or until the cheese has melted. Serve immediately with black olives, if you like.

COOK'S TIP
Treat all fresh herbs gently during preparation, as they contain volatile oils that can easily be lost. Most herbs are best added towards the end of cooking (as with this recipe), to preserve their flavour and colour.

VARIATIONS
• Use 2–3 sprigs of fresh rosemary instead of fresh mixed herbs.
• Use grated half-fat hard cheese such as Cheddar in place of mozzarella.

Energy 107Kcal/445kJ; Protein 5.2g; Carbohydrate 11.1g, of which sugars 9g; Fat 4.9g, of which saturates 2g; Cholesterol 7mg; Calcium 89mg; Fibre 2.8g; Sodium 54mg.

RATATOUILLE ★

A TOMATO AND MIXED VEGETABLE STEW FROM PROVENCE, FRANCE, THIS LOW-FAT VERSION OF RATATOUILLE IS STIRRED AND SERVED WARM OR COOL, WITH CRUSTY BREAD TO MOP UP THE JUICES.

SERVES SIX

INGREDIENTS
   900g/2lb ripe tomatoes
   30ml/2 tbsp olive oil
   2 onions, thinly sliced
   2 red and 1 yellow (bell) pepper,
     seeded and cut into chunks
   1 large aubergine (eggplant), cut
     into chunks
   2 courgettes (zucchini), sliced
   4 garlic cloves, crushed
   2 bay leaves
   15ml/1 tbsp chopped fresh thyme
   salt and ground black pepper

1 Plunge the tomatoes into a bowl of boiling water for 30 seconds, then refresh in cold water. Peel away the skins and chop the flesh roughly.

2 Heat a little of the oil in a large, heavy non-stick pan and gently cook the onions for 5 minutes. Stir them constantly so that they do not brown, as this will adversely affect their flavour and make them bitter. Cook them until they are just transparent.

3 Add the peppers to the softened onions and cook for a further 2 minutes. Using a slotted spoon, transfer the onions and peppers to a plate and set them aside.

4 Add a little more oil to the pan, add the aubergine and cook gently for 5 minutes. Add the remaining oil and courgettes, and cook for 3 minutes. Lift out the courgettes and aubergine and set them aside.

5 Add the garlic and tomatoes to the pan with the bay leaves and thyme, and a little salt and pepper. Cook gently until the tomatoes have softened and are turning pulpy.

6 Return all the vegetables to the pan and cook gently for about 15 minutes, until fairly pulpy but retaining a little texture, stirring frequently. Season to taste. Serve warm or leave to cool and chill.

Energy 115Kcal/480kJ; Protein 3.9g; Carbohydrate 14.6g, of which sugars 13.1g; Fat 4.9g, of which saturates 0.9g; Cholesterol 0mg; Calcium 49mg; Fibre 4.7g; Sodium 19mg.

BAKED MEDITERRANEAN VEGETABLES ★

CRUNCHY GOLDEN BATTER SURROUNDS THESE VEGETABLES, MAKING THEM COMFORTING AND FILLING. SERVE WITH SALAD AS A LIGHT LUNCH, OR WITH GRILLED VEGETARIAN SAUSAGES FOR A MORE HEARTY MEAL.

SERVES SIX

INGREDIENTS

1 small aubergine (eggplant),
  trimmed, halved and thickly sliced
1 egg
115g/4oz/1 cup plain
  (all-purpose) flour
300ml/½ pint/1¼ cups
  semi-skimmed (low-fat) milk
30ml/2 tbsp fresh thyme leaves,
  or 10ml/2 tsp dried thyme
1 red onion
2 large courgettes (zucchini)
1 red (bell) pepper
1 yellow (bell) pepper
30ml/2 tbsp sunflower oil
30ml/2 tbsp grated fresh Parmesan
  cheese (optional)
salt and ground black pepper
fresh herb sprigs, to serve

1 Place the aubergine in a colander or sieve (strainer), sprinkle generously with salt and leave for 10 minutes. Drain, rinse well and pat dry on kitchen paper.

2 Meanwhile, beat the egg in a bowl, then gradually mix in the flour and a little milk to make a smooth thick paste. Gradually blend in the rest of the milk, add the thyme leaves and seasoning to taste and stir until smooth. Leave the batter in a cool place until required. Preheat the oven to 220°C/425°F/Gas 7.

3 Quarter the onion, slice the courgettes and seed and quarter the peppers. Put the oil in a roasting pan and heat in the oven for a few minutes, until hot. Add the prepared vegetables, toss in the oil to coat thoroughly and return to the oven for 20 minutes.

4 Give the batter a whisk, then pour it over the vegetables. Return the pan to the oven for 30 minutes. When puffed up and golden, reduce the heat to 190°C/375°F/Gas 5 and bake for 10–15 minutes until crisp around the edges. Sprinkle with Parmesan, if using, and herbs. Serve.

COOK'S TIP
As with Yorkshire pudding, it is essential to get the oil in the dish really hot before adding the batter, which should sizzle slightly as it goes in. If the fat is not hot enough, the batter will not rise well. Use a dish that is not too deep.

Energy 151Kcal/635kJ; Protein 6.3g; Carbohydrate 23g, of which sugars 7.9g; Fat 4.4g, of which saturates 1.2g; Cholesterol 35mg; Calcium 113mg; Fibre 2.5g; Sodium 37mg.

MEDITERRANEAN VEGETABLES <u>WITH</u> CHICKPEAS ★

THE FLAVOURS OF THE MEDITERRANEAN ARE CAPTURED IN THIS EXOTIC LOW-FAT VEGETARIAN DISH, IDEAL FOR A LUNCHTIME SNACK OR LIGHT SUPPER, SERVED WITH FLATBREADS SUCH AS PITTA.

SERVES SIX

INGREDIENTS
1 onion, sliced
2 leeks, sliced
2 garlic cloves, crushed
1 red (bell) pepper, seeded
  and sliced
1 green (bell) pepper, seeded
  and sliced
1 yellow (bell) pepper, seeded
  and sliced
350g/12oz courgettes
  (zucchini), sliced
225g/8oz/3 cups mushrooms, sliced
400g/14oz can chopped tomatoes
30ml/2 tbsp ruby port or red wine
30ml/2 tbsp tomato purée (paste)
15ml/1 tbsp tomato ketchup
  (optional)
400g/14oz can chickpeas, rinsed
  and drained
115g/4oz/1 cup pitted black olives
45ml/3 tbsp chopped mixed
  fresh herbs
salt and ground black pepper
chopped mixed fresh herbs,
  to garnish

1 Put the onion, leeks, garlic, red, yellow and green peppers, courgettes and mushrooms into a large pan.

2 Add the tomatoes, port or red wine, tomato purée and tomato ketchup, if using to the pan and mix all the ingredients together well.

3 Cover, bring to the boil, then reduce the heat and simmer the mixture gently for 20–30 minutes, until the vegetables are cooked and tender but not overcooked, stirring occasionally. Stir in the rinsed chickpeas a few minutes before the end of the cooking time.

4 Remove the lid of the pan and increase the heat slightly for the last 10 minutes of the cooking time, to thicken the sauce, if you like.

5 Stir in the olives, herbs and seasoning. Serve either hot or cold, garnished with chopped mixed herbs.

Energy 161Kcal/678kJ; Protein 7.9g; Carbohydrate 21.7g, of which sugars 13.4g; Fat 4.7g, of which saturates 0.8g; Cholesterol 0mg; Calcium 78mg; Fibre 7g; Sodium 639mg.

LINGUINE WITH SUN-DRIED TOMATOES ★

CHOOSE PLAIN SUN-DRIED TOMATOES FOR THIS SAUCE, INSTEAD OF THOSE PRESERVED IN OIL, AS THEY WILL INCREASE THE FAT CONTENT. SERVE WITH A MIXED BABY LEAF SALAD FOR A TASTY LIGHT SUPPER.

SERVES FOUR

INGREDIENTS
1 garlic clove, crushed
1 celery stick, thinly sliced
115g/4oz/2 cups sun-dried tomatoes, finely chopped
90ml/6 tbsp red wine
8 fresh ripe plum tomatoes
350g/12oz dried linguine
salt and ground black pepper
fresh basil leaves, to garnish

1 Put the garlic, celery, sun-dried tomatoes and wine into a pan, and cook gently for 15 minutes.

2 Meanwhile, plunge the plum tomatoes into a separate pan of boiling water for 30 seconds, then transfer the tomatoes to a pan of cold water. Drain, then slip off their skins. Halve them, remove and discard the seeds and cores, and roughly chop the flesh.

3 Add the tomato flesh to the pan and simmer for a further 5 minutes. Season to taste with salt and pepper.

4 Meanwhile, cook the linguine in a large pan of lightly salted boiling water for 8–10 minutes, or until *al dente*. Drain well.

5 Return the pasta to the pan, add half the tomato sauce and toss to mix well. Serve immediately on warmed plates, topped with the remaining sauce, and garnished with basil leaves.

COOK'S TIP
Add shavings of fresh Parmesan for extra flavour, if you like, but remember this will add extra calories and fat.

Energy 346Kcal/1474kJ; Protein 12.1g; Carbohydrate 71.5g, of which sugars 9.6g; Fat 2.2g, of which saturates 0.4g; Cholesterol 0mg; Calcium 41mg; Fibre 4.8g; Sodium 27mg.

CLASSIC MIXED MUSHROOM RISOTTO ★

A CLASSIC LOW-FAT RISOTTO OF MIXED MUSHROOMS, HERBS AND PARMESAN CHEESE, THIS IS BEST SIMPLY SERVED WITH A MIXED LEAF SALAD TOSSED IN A LIGHT FAT-FREE DRESSING.

SERVES FOUR

INGREDIENTS
10ml/2 tsp olive oil
4 shallots, finely chopped
2 garlic cloves, crushed
10g/¼oz dried porcini mushrooms, soaked in 150ml/¼ pint/⅔ cup hot water for 20 minutes
450g/1lb/6 cups mixed mushrooms, such as closed cup, chestnut and field (portabello) mushrooms, sliced
250g/9oz/1¼ cups long grain rice
900ml/1½ pints/3¾ cups well-flavoured vegetable stock
30–45ml/2–3 tbsp chopped fresh flat leaf parsley
40g/1½oz/½ cup freshly grated Parmesan cheese (optional)
salt and ground black pepper

1 Heat the oil in a large, non-stick pan. Add the shallots and garlic and cook gently for 5 minutes, stirring constantly.

2 Drain the porcini, reserving their liquid, and chop roughly. Add all the mushrooms to the pan with the porcini soaking liquid, the rice and 300ml/½ pint/1¼ cups of the stock.

3 Bring to the boil, then reduce the heat and simmer uncovered until all the liquid has been absorbed, stirring frequently. Add a ladleful of hot stock and stir until it has been absorbed.

4 Continue cooking and adding the hot stock, a ladleful at a time, until the rice is cooked and creamy but *al dente*, stirring frequently. This should take about 35 minutes and it may not be necessary to add all the stock.

5 Season to taste with salt and pepper, then stir in the chopped parsley and grated Parmesan, if using. Serve at once. Alternatively, sprinkle the Parmesan, if using, over the risotto just before serving.

Energy 256Kcal/1071kJ; Protein 7g; Carbohydrate 50.5g, of which sugars 0.3g; Fat 2.6g, of which saturates 0.4g; Cholesterol 0mg; Calcium 20mg; Fibre 1.4g; Sodium 132mg.

LENTIL DHAL WITH ROASTED GARLIC ★

THIS DHAL MAKES A COMFORTING LIGHT MEAL WHEN SERVED WITH BROWN RICE OR LOW-FAT INDIAN BREADS AND ANY DRY-SPICED VEGETARIAN DISH, PARTICULARLY A CAULIFLOWER OR POTATO DISH.

SERVES SIX

INGREDIENTS

15g/½oz/1 tbsp butter or ghee
1 onion, chopped
2 fresh green chillies, seeded and chopped
15ml/1 tbsp chopped fresh root ginger
225g/8oz/1 cup yellow or red lentils
900ml/1½ pints/3¾ cups water
45ml/3 tbsp roasted garlic purée (paste)
5ml/1 tsp ground cumin
5ml/1 tsp ground coriander
200g/7oz tomatoes, skinned and diced
a little lemon juice
salt and ground black pepper
30–45ml/2–3 tbsp fresh coriander (cilantro) sprigs, to garnish

COOK'S TIP
Mustard seeds (both yellow and black ones) are widely used in Indian dishes such as this one, to add a delicious flavour and texture. The yellow seeds are milder than the black ones.

For the spicy garnish
10ml/2 tsp sunflower oil
4–5 shallots, sliced
2 garlic cloves, thinly sliced
15g/½oz/1 tbsp butter or ghee
5ml/1 tsp cumin seeds
5ml/1 tsp mustard seeds
3–4 small dried red chillies
8–10 fresh curry leaves

1 First begin the spicy garnish. Heat the oil in a large, heavy, non-stick pan. Add the shallots and cook them over a medium heat for 5–10 minutes until they are crisp and browned, stirring occasionally. Add the garlic and cook for a moment or two until the garlic colours slightly, stirring frequently. Remove the pan from the heat and use a slotted spoon to remove the shallots and garlic from the pan. Set aside.

2 Melt the butter or ghee for the dhal in the pan, add the onion, chillies and ginger, and cook for 10 minutes until golden.

3 Stir in the yellow or red lentils and water, then bring to the boil, reduce the heat and part-cover the pan. Simmer for 50–60 minutes until it is the same consistency as a very thick soup, stirring occasionally.

4 Stir in the roasted garlic purée, cumin and ground coriander, then season to taste with salt and pepper. Cook the dhal, uncovered, for a further 10–15 minutes, stirring frequently.

5 Stir in the tomatoes, then adjust the seasoning, adding a little lemon juice to taste, if necessary.

6 To finish the spicy garnish: melt the butter or ghee in a non-stick frying pan. Add the cumin and mustard seeds and cook until the mustard seeds begin to pop. Stir in the dried red chillies and fresh curry leaves, then immediately swirl the mixture into the cooked dhal. Garnish with coriander sprigs and the spicy fried shallots and garlic. Serve.

Energy 147Kcal/623kJ; Protein 9.3g; Carbohydrate 23g, of which sugars 2.5g; Fat 2.7g, of which saturates 1.4g; Cholesterol 5mg; Calcium 24mg; Fibre 2.3g; Sodium 32mg.

FRIED RICE WITH MUSHROOMS ★

A TASTY LOW-FAT VERSION OF THIS POPULAR CHINESE DISH. YOU CAN ADD DIFFERENT VEGETABLES,
IF YOU LIKE — GREEN BEANS, BROCCOLI OR PEAS WOULD ALL WORK WELL.

SERVES FOUR

INGREDIENTS
225g/8oz/generous 1 cup long
  grain rice
10ml/2 tsp vegetable oil
1 egg, lightly beaten
2 garlic cloves, crushed
175g/6oz/scant 2½ cups button
  (white) mushrooms, sliced
15ml/1 tbsp light soy sauce
1.5ml/¼ tsp salt
2.5ml/½ tsp sesame oil
cucumber matchsticks, to garnish

1 Rinse the rice until the water runs clear, then drain thoroughly. Place it in a pan. Measure the depth of the rice against your index finger, then bring the finger up to just above the surface of the rice and add cold water to the same depth as the rice.

2 Bring the water to the boil. Stir, boil for a few minutes, then cover the pan. Reduce the heat to a simmer and cook the rice gently for 5–8 minutes, until all the water has been absorbed. Remove the pan from the heat and, without lifting the lid, leave for a further 10 minutes before stirring or forking up the rice. Leave to cool.

COOK'S TIP
When you cook rice this way, you may find there is a crust at the bottom of the pan. Don't worry; simply soak the crust in water for a couple of minutes to break it up, then drain it and fry it with the rest of the rice.

3 Heat 5ml/1 tsp of the vegetable oil in a non-stick frying pan or wok. Add the egg and cook until scrambled, stirring with chopsticks or wooden spoon. Remove the egg to a plate and set aside.

4 Heat the remaining vegetable oil in the pan or wok. Stir-fry the garlic for a few seconds, then add the mushrooms and stir-fry for 2 minutes, adding a little water, if needed, to prevent burning.

5 Stir in the cooled rice and cook for about 4 minutes, or until the rice is hot, stirring occasionally.

6 Add the scrambled egg, soy sauce, salt and sesame oil. Cook for 1 minute to heat through. Serve immediately, garnished with cucumber matchsticks.

Energy 245Kcal/1022kJ; Protein 6.6g; Carbohydrate 45.4g, of which sugars 0.4g; Fat 3.8g, of which saturates 0.7g; Cholesterol 48mg; Calcium 21mg; Fibre 0.5g; Sodium 287mg.

MAIN MEALS

Some vegetarian main meals can be quite high in calories and fat, and can eat into your daily calorie and fat limits. But be reassured: the main dishes included here are low in fat (almost all containing 10g of fat or less per serving) while still being full of flavour. The following versatile collection includes classic favourites such as Vegetable Moussaka and Red Pepper Risotto.

LEEK, SQUASH AND TOMATO GRATIN ★★

COLOURFUL AND SUCCULENT, YOU CAN USE VIRTUALLY ANY KIND OF SQUASH FOR THIS DELICIOUS, LOW-FAT AUTUMN GRATIN, FROM PATTY PANS AND ACORN SQUASH TO PUMPKINS.

SERVES SIX

INGREDIENTS

    450g/1lb peeled and seeded squash,
      cut into 1cm/½in slices
    20ml/4 tsp olive oil
    450g/1lb leeks, cut into thick,
      diagonal slices
    675g/1½lb tomatoes, skinned and
      thickly sliced
    2.5ml/½ tsp ground toasted cumin seeds
    175ml/6fl oz/¾ cup single
      (light) cream
    120ml/4fl oz/½ cup vegetable stock
    1 fresh red chilli, seeded and sliced
    1 garlic clove, finely chopped
    15ml/1 tbsp chopped fresh mint
    30ml/2 tbsp chopped fresh parsley
    60ml/4 tbsp fresh white breadcrumbs
    salt and ground black pepper

1 Steam the squash over a pan of boiling water for 10 minutes.

2 Heat half the oil in a non-stick frying pan and cook the leeks gently for 5–6 minutes until lightly coloured. Try to keep the slices intact. Preheat the oven to 190°C/375°F/Gas 5.

3 Layer all the squash, leeks and tomatoes in a 2 litre/3½ pint/8 cup gratin dish, arranging them in rows. Season with salt, pepper and cumin.

4 Pour the cream and stock into a small pan and add the chilli and garlic. Bring to the boil over a low heat, stirring, then stir in the mint. Pour the mixture evenly over the layered vegetables, using a rubber spatula to scrape all the sauce out of the pan.

5 Bake in the oven for 50–55 minutes, or until the gratin is bubbling and tinged brown. Sprinkle the parsley and breadcrumbs on top and drizzle over the remaining oil. Bake for a further 15–20 minutes until the breadcrumbs are browned and crisp. Serve immediately.

VARIATION
For a curried version, use ground coriander as well as cumin, and coconut milk instead of cream. Use fresh coriander (cilantro) instead of mint and parsley.

Energy 157Kcal/660kJ; Protein 4.8g; Carbohydrate 15.9g, of which sugars 7.5g; Fat 8.7g, of which saturates 4.1g; Cholesterol 16mg; Calcium 100mg; Fibre 4.1g; Sodium 98mg.

RICH VEGETABLE HOT-POT ★★

HERE'S A ONE-DISH MEAL THAT'S SUITABLE FOR FEEDING LARGE NUMBERS OF PEOPLE. IT'S LIGHTLY SPICED, LOW IN FAT AND HAS PLENTY OF GARLIC TOO — WHO COULD REFUSE?

SERVES FOUR

INGREDIENTS
- 30ml/2 tbsp extra virgin olive oil or sunflower oil
- 1 large onion, chopped
- 2 small–medium aubergines (eggplants), cut into small cubes
- 4 courgettes (zucchini), cut into small chunks
- 2 red, yellow or green (bell) peppers, seeded and chopped
- 115g/4oz/1 cup fresh or frozen peas
- 115g/4oz green beans
- 200g/7oz can flageolet (small cannellini) beans, rinsed and drained
- 450g/1lb new or salad potatoes, peeled and diced
- 2.5ml/½ tsp ground cinnamon
- 2.5ml/½ tsp ground cumin
- 5ml/1 tsp paprika
- 4–5 fresh tomatoes, skinned
- 400g/14oz can chopped tomatoes
- 30ml/2 tbsp chopped fresh parsley
- 3–4 garlic cloves, crushed
- 350ml/12fl oz/1½ cups vegetable stock
- salt and ground black pepper
- black olives, to garnish
- fresh parsley, to garnish

1 Preheat the oven to 190°C/375°F/ Gas 5. Heat 15ml/1 tbsp of the oil in a heavy, non-stick pan, and cook the onion until golden. Add the aubergines, cook for 3 minutes, then add the courgettes, peppers, peas, beans and potatoes, and stir in the spices and seasoning. Cook for 3 minutes, stirring constantly.

2 Cut the fresh tomatoes in half and scoop out the seeds. Chop the tomatoes finely and place them in a bowl. Stir in the canned tomatoes with the chopped parsley, garlic and the remaining olive oil. Spoon the aubergine mixture into a shallow ovenproof dish and level the surface.

3 Pour the stock over the aubergine mixture, then spoon the prepared tomato mixture over the top.

4 Cover the dish with foil and bake in the oven for 30–45 minutes until the vegetables are tender. Serve hot, garnished with black olives and parsley.

Energy 310Kcal/1303kJ; Protein 12.9g; Carbohydrate 49.3g, of which sugars 20.4g; Fat 8.2g, of which saturates 1.3g; Cholesterol 0mg; Calcium 124mg; Fibre 12.1g; Sodium 225mg.

VEGETABLE MOUSSAKA ★★

THIS IS A REALLY FLAVOURSOME AND LOW-FAT VEGETARIAN ALTERNATIVE TO CLASSIC MEAT MOUSSAKA.
SERVE IT WITH WARM BREAD AND A GLASS OR TWO OF RUSTIC RED WINE.

SERVES SIX

INGREDIENTS
  450g/1lb aubergines (eggplants),
    sliced
  115g/4oz/½ cup whole green lentils
  600ml/1 pint/2½ cups vegetable stock
  1 bay leaf
  225g/8oz tomatoes
  25ml/5 tsp olive oil
  1 onion, sliced
  1 garlic clove, crushed
  225g/8oz/3 cups mushrooms, sliced
  400g/14oz can chickpeas, rinsed
    and drained
  400g/14oz can chopped tomatoes
  30ml/2 tbsp tomato purée (paste)
  10ml/2 tsp dried basil
  300ml/½ pint/1¼ cups low-fat
    natural (plain) yogurt
  3 eggs
  50g/2oz/½ cup reduced-fat mature
    (sharp) Cheddar cheese, grated
  salt and ground black pepper
  fresh flat leaf parsley sprigs,
    to garnish

1 Sprinkle the aubergine slices with
salt and place in a colander. Cover and
leave for 30 minutes to allow any bitter
juices to be extracted.

2 Meanwhile, place the lentils, stock
and bay leaf in a pan. Cover, bring to
the boil and simmer for about
20 minutes until the lentils are just
tender. Drain well and keep warm.

3 If you like, skin the fresh tomatoes
then cut them into pieces.

4 Heat 10ml/2 tsp of the oil in a large,
non-stick pan, add the onion and garlic,
and cook for 5 minutes, stirring. Stir in
the lentils, mushrooms, chickpeas, fresh
and canned tomatoes, tomato purée,
basil and 45ml/3 tbsp water. Bring to
the boil, cover and simmer gently for
10 minutes.

5 Preheat the oven to 180°C/350°F/
Gas 4. Rinse the aubergine slices, drain
and pat dry. Heat the remaining oil in a
non-stick frying pan and cook the
aubergines in batches for 3–4 minutes,
turning once.

VARIATIONS
Use 5–10ml/1–2 tsp mixed dried herbs
in place of dried basil. Use other
reduced-fat hard cheese such as Red
Leicester in place of Cheddar. Use fresh
Parmesan cheese in place of Cheddar,
but remember this will increase the
calorie and fat contents of the dish.

6 Season the lentil mixture. Layer the
aubergines and lentils in an ovenproof
dish, starting with aubergines and
finishing with the lentil mixture.

7 Beat together the yogurt, eggs and
salt and pepper, and pour the mixture
evenly into the dish. Sprinkle the cheese
on top. Bake in the oven for 45 minutes.
Serve, garnished with parsley sprigs.

Energy 768Kcal/3255kJ; Protein 60.2g; Carbohydrate 109.6g, of which sugars 10.3g; Fat 13.1g, of which saturates 2.9g; Cholesterol 99mg; Calcium 357mg; Fibre 21.8g; Sodium 320mg.

LENTIL FRITTATA ★★

OMELETTES TEND TO HAVE THE EGG MIXTURE COOKED AND FOLDED AROUND A FILLING, WHILE A FRITTATA JUST MIXES IT ALL UP. THIS RECIPE COMBINES GREEN LENTILS, RED ONIONS, BROCCOLI AND TOMATOES.

SERVES EIGHT

INGREDIENTS
   75g/3oz/scant ½ cup green lentils
   225g/8oz small broccoli florets
   2 red onions, halved and thickly sliced
   15ml/1 tbsp olive oil
   8 eggs
   45ml/3 tbsp water
   45ml/3 tbsp chopped mixed fresh
      herbs, such as oregano, parsley,
      tarragon and chives, plus extra
      sprigs to garnish
   175g/6oz cherry tomatoes, halved
   salt and ground black pepper

1 Place the lentils in a pan, cover with cold water and bring to the boil, then reduce the heat and simmer for 25 minutes until tender. Add the broccoli, return to the boil and cook for 1 minute.

VARIATIONS
Use green beans, halved, in place of broccoli florets. Use standard white onions in place of red onions.

2 Meanwhile place the onion slices and olive oil in a shallow earthenware dish or cazuela about 23–25cm/9–10in in diameter, and place in a cold (unheated) oven. Set the oven to 200°C/400°F/Gas 6 and cook for 25 minutes.

3 In a bowl, whisk together the eggs, water, a pinch of salt and plenty of pepper. Stir in the chopped herbs and set aside.

4 Drain the lentils and broccoli and stir into the onions. Add the cherry tomatoes and stir gently to combine.

5 Pour the egg mixture evenly over the vegetables. Reduce the oven temperature to 190°C/375°F/Gas 5. Return the dish to the oven and cook for 10 minutes, then push the mixture into the centre of the dish using a spatula, allowing the raw egg mixture in the centre to flow to the edges.

6 Return the dish to the oven and cook the frittata for a further 15 minutes, or until it is just set. Garnish with sprigs of fresh herbs and serve warm, cut into wedges.

Energy 145Kcal/605kJ; Protein 10.5g; Carbohydrate 9.7g, of which sugars 4g; Fat 7.5g, of which saturates 1.8g; Cholesterol 190mg; Calcium 65mg; Fibre 2.5g; Sodium 77mg.

BAKED CHEESE POLENTA WITH TOMATO SAUCE ★★

POLENTA, OR CORNMEAL, IS A STAPLE FOOD IN ITALY THAT IS LOW IN FAT. IT IS COOKED NOT UNLIKE A PORRIDGE, AND EATEN SOFT, OR SET AND CUT INTO SHAPES THEN BAKED OR GRILLED.

SERVES FOUR

INGREDIENTS
5ml/1 tsp salt
250g/9oz/2¼ cups quick-cook
 polenta
5ml/1 tsp paprika
2.5ml/½ tsp freshly grated nutmeg
10ml/2 tsp olive oil
1 large onion, finely chopped
2 garlic cloves, crushed
2 x 400g/14oz cans chopped
 tomatoes
15ml/1 tbsp tomato purée (paste)
5ml/1 tsp granulated sugar
salt and ground black pepper
75g/3oz/¾ cup Gruyère cheese,
 finely grated

1 Lightly grease an ovenproof dish and set aside. Line a 28 x 18cm/11 x 7in baking tin (pan) with clear film (plastic wrap). In a pan, bring 1 litre/1¾ pints/ 4 cups water to the boil with the salt.

2 Pour in the polenta in a steady stream and cook, stirring continuously, for 5 minutes. Beat in the paprika and nutmeg, then pour the mixture into the prepared tin and smooth the surface. Leave to cool.

3 Heat the oil in a non-stick pan and cook the onion and garlic until they go soft. Add the tomatoes, tomato purée and sugar. Season to taste with salt and pepper. Bring to the boil, then reduce the heat and allow the mixture to simmer for about 20 minutes.

4 Meanwhile, preheat the oven to 200°C/400°F/Gas 6. Turn out the polenta on to a chopping board, and cut into 5cm/2in squares. Place half the squares in the prepared ovenproof dish. Spoon over half the tomato sauce, and sprinkle with half the cheese. Repeat the layers. Bake in the oven for about 25 minutes, or until golden. Serve hot.

Energy 369Kcal/1548kJ; Protein 14.6g; Carbohydrate 61.4g, of which sugars 13.4g; Fat 7.2g, of which saturates 2.2g; Cholesterol 8mg; Calcium 200mg; Fibre 4.9g; Sodium 647mg.

HERB POLENTA WITH GRILLED TOMATOES ★

Golden polenta flavoured with fresh summer herbs and served with sweet grilled tomatoes creates this tasty low-fat Italian dish, ideal for lunch or supper.

4 Remove the pan from the heat and stir in the butter, chopped herbs and pepper.

5 Transfer the polenta mixture to a wide, lightly greased dish or baking tin (pan) and spread it out evenly. Leave until it is completely cool and has set.

6 Turn the polenta out on to a chopping board and cut it into squares or stamp out rounds with a large biscuit cutter. Lightly brush the squares or rounds with oil.

7 Lightly brush the tomatoes with oil and sprinkle with salt and pepper.

8 Cook the tomatoes and polenta over a medium hot barbecue or under a preheated grill (broiler) for 5 minutes, turning once. Serve hot, garnished with herbs.

SERVES SIX

INGREDIENTS
750ml/1¼ pints/3 cups vegetable stock or water
5ml/1 tsp salt
175g/6oz/1½ cups polenta
15g/½oz/1 tbsp butter
75ml/5 tbsp chopped mixed fresh parsley, chives and basil, plus extra to garnish
10ml/2 tsp olive oil
4 large plum or beefsteak tomatoes, halved
salt and ground black pepper

1 Prepare the polenta in advance: place the stock or water in a pan with the salt, and bring to the boil.

2 Reduce the heat and gradually add the polenta, stirring constantly to ensure that it doesn't form any lumps.

3 Stir constantly over a medium heat for 5 minutes, until the polenta begins to thicken and comes away from the sides of the pan.

VARIATION
Any mixture of fresh herbs can be used, or try using just basil or chives alone, for a really distinctive flavour.

Energy 146Kcal/611kJ; Protein 3.2g; Carbohydrate 23.4g, of which sugars 2.1g; Fat 4.2g, of which saturates 1.5g; Cholesterol 5mg; Calcium 6mg; Fibre 1.3g; Sodium 349mg.

FUSILLI <u>WITH</u> BASIL <u>AND</u> PEPPERS ★★

CHARGRILLED PEPPERS HAVE A WONDERFUL, SMOKY FLAVOUR THAT MARRIES WELL WITH GARLIC, OLIVES, BASIL AND TOMATOES IN THIS DELECTABLE LOW-FAT PASTA DISH.

SERVES FOUR

INGREDIENTS
3 large (bell) peppers (red, yellow and orange)
350g/12oz/3 cups fresh or dried fusilli
30ml/2 tbsp extra virgin olive oil
1–2 garlic cloves, to taste, finely chopped
4 ripe plum tomatoes, skinned, seeded and diced
50g/2oz/½ cup pitted black olives, halved or quartered lengthways
a handful of fresh basil leaves
salt and ground black pepper

VARIATION
Use vine-ripened tomatoes in place of plum tomatoes.

1 Put the whole peppers under a hot grill (broiler) and cook for about 10 minutes, until charred on all sides, turning frequently.

2 Put the hot peppers in a plastic bag, seal the bag and set aside until the peppers are cold.

3 Remove the peppers from the bag and hold them, one at a time, under cold running water. Peel off the charred skins with your fingers, split the peppers open and pull out the cores. Rub off all the seeds under the running water, then pat the peppers dry on kitchen paper.

4 Cook the pasta in a pan of salted boiling water until *al dente*.

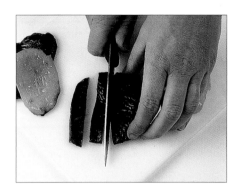

5 Meanwhile, thinly slice the peppers and place them in a large bowl with the olive oil, garlic, tomatoes, olives and basil. Add salt and pepper to taste.

6 Drain the cooked pasta and transfer it to the bowl with the other ingredients. Toss well to mix and serve immediately.

Energy 420Kcal/1778kJ; Protein 12.6g; Carbohydrate 76.4g, of which sugars 14g; Fat 9.3g, of which saturates 1.4g; Cholesterol 0mg; Calcium 46mg; Fibre 6g; Sodium 297mg.

PASTA, SUN-DRIED TOMATOES AND RADICCHIO ★★

USE PAGLIA E FIENO *PASTA TO GET THE BEST FROM THIS MODERN PASTA DISH. CAREFUL DRIZZLING OF THE TOMATO SAUCE AND PLACING OF THE PASTA ARE KEY TO THIS RECIPE.*

SERVES SIX

INGREDIENTS
45ml/3 tbsp pine nuts
350g/12oz *paglia e fieno* (or two
  different colours of tagliatelle)
30ml/2 tbsp extra virgin olive oil or
  sunflower oil
30ml/2 tbsp sun-dried tomato paste
2 pieces drained sun-dried tomatoes
  in olive oil, cut into very
  thin slivers
40g/1½oz radicchio leaves,
  finely shredded
4–6 spring onions (scallions), thinly
  sliced into rings
salt and ground black pepper

1 Put the pine nuts in a non-stick frying pan and toss over a low to medium heat for 1–2 minutes, or until they are lightly toasted and golden. Remove from the heat and set aside.

2 Cook the pasta according to the packet instructions, keeping the colours separate by using two pans.

3 While the pasta is cooking, heat 15ml/1 tbsp of the oil in a non-stick pan or frying pan. Add the sun-dried tomato paste and the sun-dried tomatoes, then stir in 2 ladlefuls of the water used for cooking the pasta. Simmer until the sauce is slightly reduced, stirring constantly.

4 Mix in the radicchio, then taste and season with salt and pepper, if necessary. Keep on a low heat. Drain the *paglia e fieno*, keeping the colours separate, and return the pasta to the pans. Add about 7.5ml/1½ tsp oil to each pan and toss over a medium to high heat until the pasta is glistening with the oil.

5 Arrange portions of green and white pasta side by side in each of 6 warmed bowls, then spoon the sun-dried tomato and radicchio mixture in the centre. Sprinkle the spring onions and pine nuts over the top and serve immediately. Before eating, each diner should toss the sauce ingredients with the pasta.

COOK'S TIP
If you find the presentation too fussy, you can toss the tomato and radicchio mixture with the pasta in a large bowl before serving, then sprinkle the spring onions and toasted pine nuts on top.

Energy 293Kcal/1237kJ; Protein 8.7g; Carbohydrate 45.1g, of which sugars 3.7g; Fat 10g, of which saturates 1g; Cholesterol 0mg; Calcium 24mg; Fibre 2.3g; Sodium 23mg.

TAGLIATELLE WITH FRESH HERBS ★★

FRESH ROSEMARY, PARSLEY, MINT, SAGE, BASIL, BAY AND GARLIC ARE ALL HERE, MERGING TOGETHER TO CREATE AN AROMATIC PASTA DISH THAT IS PACKED WITH TASTE.

SERVES SIX

INGREDIENTS

3 fresh rosemary sprigs
1 small handful fresh flat leaf parsley
5–6 fresh mint leaves
5–6 fresh sage leaves
8–10 large fresh basil leaves
30ml/2 tbsp extra virgin olive oil
25g/1oz/2 tbsp butter
1 shallot, finely chopped
2 garlic cloves, finely chopped
a pinch of chilli powder, to taste
400g/14oz fresh egg tagliatelle
1 bay leaf
120ml/4fl oz/½ cup dry white wine
90–120ml/6–8 tbsp vegetable stock
salt and ground black pepper
fresh basil leaves, to garnish

1 Strip the rosemary and parsley leaves from their stalks and chop them together with the other fresh herbs.

2 Heat the oil and half the butter in a large non-stick pan. Add the shallot, garlic and chilli powder. Cook over a very low heat for 2–3 minutes, stirring frequently.

3 Meanwhile, cook the fresh pasta in a large pan of salted boiling water according to the packet instructions.

4 Add the chopped herbs and the bay leaf to the shallot mixture and cook for 2–3 minutes, stirring, then add the wine and increase the heat. Boil rapidly for 1–2 minutes, or until reduced. Reduce the heat, add the stock and simmer gently for 1–2 minutes. Season.

5 Drain the pasta and add it to the herb mixture. Toss well to mix and remove and discard the bay leaf.

6 Put the remaining butter in a warmed large bowl, transfer the dressed pasta to it and toss well to mix. Serve immediately, garnished with basil.

Energy 289Kcal/1223kJ; Protein 8.5g; Carbohydrate 50.7g, of which sugars 3.2g; Fat 5.8g, of which saturates 2.5g; Cholesterol 9mg; Calcium 47mg; Fibre 2.7g; Sodium 33mg.

GRILLED VEGETABLE PIZZA ★★

YOU REALLY CAN'T GO TOO FAR WRONG WITH THIS CLASSIC MIXTURE OF GRILLED VEGETABLES ON HOME-MADE PIZZA DOUGH. IT IS LOW IN FAT, AND LOOKS AND TASTES GREAT TOO.

3 Place the pizza dough on a sheet of baking parchment on top of a baking sheet, and roll or gently press it out to form a 25cm/10in round, making the edges slightly thicker than the centre.

4 Lightly brush the pizza dough with any remaining oil, then spread the chopped plum tomatoes evenly over the dough.

5 Sprinkle with the chopped basil and season with salt and pepper. Arrange the grilled vegetables over the tomatoes and top with the cheese.

6 Bake in the oven for 25–30 minutes until crisp and golden brown. Garnish the pizza with fresh basil sprigs and serve immediately, cut into slices.

SERVES EIGHT

INGREDIENTS
1 courgette (zucchini), sliced
2 baby aubergines (eggplants) or
  1 small aubergine, sliced
15ml/1 tbsp olive oil
1 yellow (bell) pepper, seeded
  and sliced
115g/4oz/1 cup cornmeal
50g/2oz/½ cup potato flour
50g/2oz/½ cup soya flour
5ml/1 tsp baking powder
2.5ml/½ tsp sea salt
50g/2oz/¼ cup butter or
  non-hydrogenated margarine
about 105ml/7 tbsp semi-skimmed
  (low-fat) milk
4 plum tomatoes, skinned
  and chopped
30ml/2 tbsp chopped fresh basil
115g/4oz half-fat mozzarella
  cheese, sliced
salt and ground black pepper
fresh basil sprigs, to garnish

1 Preheat the grill (broiler) to high. Brush the courgette and aubergine slices with a little oil and place on a grill (broiler) rack with the pepper slices. Cook under the grill until lightly browned, turning once.

2 Meanwhile, preheat the oven to 200°C/400°F/Gas 6. Place the cornmeal, potato flour, soya flour, baking powder and sea salt in a mixing bowl and stir to mix. Lightly rub in the butter or margarine until the mixture resembles coarse breadcrumbs, then stir in enough of the milk to make a soft but not sticky dough.

COOK'S TIP
This recipe uses a combination of different types of flours to give an interesting flavour and texture to the base. If you prefer, use 225g/8oz/ 2 cups of plain (all-purpose) flour or a combination of half plain and half wholemeal (whole-wheat) flours.

VARIATION
Top the pizza with 115g/4oz sliced chèvre cheese (goat's cheese) instead of the mozzarella for a creamy alternative. Remember, this will increase the calorie and fat contents of the recipe.

Energy 217Kcal/907kJ; Protein 12g; Carbohydrate 20.7g, of which sugars 8.1g; Fat 9.7g, of which saturates 4.4g; Cholesterol 16mg; Calcium 114mg; Fibre 4.7g; Sodium 74mg.

TOMATO AND OLIVE MINI PIZZAS ★★

FOR A QUICK AND LIGHT VEGETARIAN SUPPER, TRY THESE DELICIOUS LITTLE PIZZAS MADE WITH FRESH AND SUN-DRIED TOMATOES. SERVE SIMPLY WITH A MIXED LEAF SIDE SALAD.

MAKES FOUR

INGREDIENTS
  150g/5oz packet of pizza base mix
  8 halves sun-dried tomatoes in olive oil, drained
  50g/2oz/½ cup pitted black olives
  1 ripe beefsteak tomato, sliced
  50g/2oz/¼ cup chèvre cheese (goat's cheese)
  30ml/2 tbsp fresh basil leaves

3 Place the sun-dried tomatoes and olives in a blender or food processor and process until smooth. Spread the mixture evenly over the pizza bases.

4 Top with the tomato slices, then crumble over the chèvre cheese. Bake in the oven for 10–15 minutes. Sprinkle with the fresh basil and serve immediately.

1 Preheat the oven to 200°C/400°F/ Gas 6. Lightly oil 2 baking sheets and set aside. Make up the pizza base following the instructions on the packet.

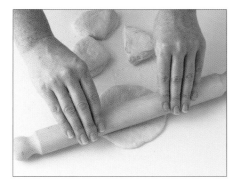

2 Divide the dough into four equal portions and roll out each portion of dough to form a 13cm/5in round. Place on the oiled baking sheets.

COOK'S TIP
You could use loose sun-dried tomatoes (preserved without oil) instead. Leave in a bowl of warm water for 10–15 minutes to soften, then drain and process with the olives.

Energy 195Kcal/823kJ; Protein 6.8g; Carbohydrate 29.9g, of which sugars 3.2g; Fat 6.2g, of which saturates 2.7g; Cholesterol 12mg; Calcium 80mg; Fibre 2.1g; Sodium 385mg.

SPINACH WITH BEANS, RAISINS AND PINE NUTS ★★

THIS LIGHT VEGETARIAN DISH IS TRADITIONALLY MADE WITH CHICKPEAS, BUT CAN ALSO BE MADE WITH HARICOT BEANS AS HERE. USE EITHER DRIED OR CANNED BEANS.

SERVES FOUR

INGREDIENTS

115g/4oz/⅔ cup haricot (navy) beans, soaked overnight, or 400g/14oz can haricot beans, rinsed and drained
30ml/2 tbsp olive oil
1 thick slice white bread
1 onion, chopped
3–4 tomatoes, skinned, seeded and chopped
2.5ml/½ tsp ground cumin
450g/1lb fresh spinach leaves
5ml/1 tsp paprika
1 garlic clove, halved
25g/1oz/generous ¼ cup raisins
15g/½oz pine nuts, toasted
salt and ground black pepper

1 Cook the dried beans in a pan of boiling water for about 1 hour, or until tender. Drain and set aside.

2 Heat 10ml/2 tsp of the oil in a non-stick frying pan and cook the bread until golden all over. Transfer to a plate and set aside.

3 Cook the onion in a further 10ml/2 tsp of the oil over a gentle heat, until soft but not brown, then add the tomatoes and cumin and continue cooking over a gentle heat.

4 Meanwhile, wash the spinach thoroughly, removing any tough stalks. Heat the remaining oil in a large, non-stick pan, stir in the paprika, then add the spinach and 45ml/3 tbsp water. Cover and cook for a few minutes, or until the spinach has wilted.

5 Add the onion and tomato mixture to the spinach and stir in the haricot beans, then season to taste with salt and pepper.

6 Place the garlic and fried bread in a blender or food processor and process until smooth. Stir the bread mixture into the spinach and bean mixture, together with the raisins. Add 175ml/6fl oz/¾ cup water and bring to the boil, then reduce the heat, cover and simmer very gently for 20–30 minutes, adding more water, if necessary.

7 Place the spinach mixture on a warmed serving plate and sprinkle with toasted pine nuts. Serve hot with Moroccan bread or other fresh bread.

Energy 231Kcal/969kJ; Protein 11.4g; Carbohydrate 25.8g, of which sugars 10.2g; Fat 9.8g, of which saturates 1.2g; Cholesterol 0mg; Calcium 240mg; Fibre 8.1g; Sodium 209mg.

MEXICAN RICE ★★

VERSIONS OF THIS DISH — A RELATIVE OF SPANISH RICE — ARE POPULAR ALL OVER SOUTH AMERICA. IT IS A TASTY LOW-FAT MEDLEY OF RICE, TOMATOES AND FRESH CHILLIES, IDEAL FOR VEGETARIANS.

SERVES SIX

INGREDIENTS

   200g/7oz/1 cup long grain rice
   400g/14oz can chopped tomatoes
   ½ onion, roughly chopped
   2 garlic cloves, roughly chopped
   15ml/1 tbsp olive oil
   225ml/7½fl oz/scant 1 cup
     vegetable stock
   2.5ml/½ tsp salt
   3 fresh red or green chillies
   150g/5oz/generous 1 cup frozen peas
   ground black pepper

1 Put the rice in a large heatproof bowl and pour over boiling water to cover. Stir once, then leave to stand for 10 minutes. Transfer to a strainer over the sink, rinse under cold water, then drain again. Set aside to dry slightly.

2 Meanwhile, pour the canned tomatoes into a blender or food processor, add the onion and garlic and process until smooth.

3 Heat the oil in a large, heavy, non-stick pan, add the rice and cook over a medium heat until the rice becomes a delicate golden brown colour. Stir occasionally with a wooden spatula to ensure that the rice does not stick to the base of the pan.

4 Add the tomato mixture and stir over a medium heat until all the liquid has been absorbed. Stir in the stock, salt, whole chillies and peas. Continue to cook the mixture until all the liquid has been absorbed and the rice is just tender, stirring occasionally.

5 Remove the pan from the heat, cover it with a tight-fitting lid and leave it to stand in a warm place for 5–10 minutes. Remove the chillies, fluff up the rice lightly with a fork, and serve in warmed bowls, sprinkled with black pepper. The chillies may be used as a garnish, if you like.

COOK'S TIP
Do not stir the rice too often after adding the stock or the grains will break down and the mixture will become starchy.

Energy 186Kcal/778kJ; Protein 5.3g; Carbohydrate 35.4g, of which sugars 5.5g; Fat 2.7g, of which saturates 0.4g; Cholesterol 0mg; Calcium 29mg; Fibre 2.6g; Sodium 8mg.

LEEK, MUSHROOM AND LEMON RISOTTO ★★

THE DELICIOUS COMBINATION OF LEEKS AND LEMON IS PERFECT IN THIS LIGHT VEGETARIAN RISOTTO.
BROWN CAP MUSHROOMS PROVIDE ADDITIONAL TEXTURE AND EXTRA FLAVOUR.

SERVES FOUR

INGREDIENTS
   225g/8oz trimmed leeks
   225g/8oz/3 cups brown cap
   (cremini) mushrooms
   15ml/1 tbsp olive oil
   3 garlic cloves, crushed
   25g/1oz/2 tbsp butter
   1 large onion, coarsely chopped
   350g/12oz/1¾ cups risotto rice, such
   as arborio or carnaroli
   1.2 litres/2 pints/5 cups simmering
   vegetable stock
   finely grated rind of 1 lemon
   45ml/3 tbsp lemon juice
   25g/1oz/⅓ cup freshly grated
   Parmesan cheese
   60ml/4 tbsp mixed chopped fresh
   chives and flat leaf parsley
   salt and ground black pepper

1 Slice the leeks in half lengthways, wash them well and then slice them evenly. Wipe the mushrooms with kitchen paper and chop them coarsely.

COOK'S TIP
Risotto rice is a rounder grain than long grain and is capable of absorbing a lot of liquid, which gives it a creamy texture.

2 Heat the oil in a large, non-stick pan and cook the garlic for 1 minute. Add the leeks, mushrooms and plenty of seasoning and cook over a medium heat for about 10 minutes, or until the leeks have softened and browned. Spoon into a bowl and set aside.

3 Add 15g/½oz/1 tbsp of the butter to the pan. When it has melted, add the onion and cook over a medium heat for 5 minutes, or until it has softened and is golden.

4 Stir in the rice and cook for about 1 minute, or until the grains begin to look translucent and are coated in the fat. Add a ladleful of stock and cook gently, until the liquid has been absorbed, stirring occasionally.

5 Continue to add stock, a ladleful at a time, until all of it has been absorbed, stirring constantly. This will take about 30 minutes. The risotto will become thick and creamy, and the rice should be tender, but not sticky.

6 Just before serving, add the leeks and mushrooms with the remaining butter. Stir in the grated lemon rind and juice. Add the Parmesan cheese and the herbs. Adjust the seasoning, if necessary and serve immediately.

Energy 442Kcal/1844kJ; Protein 11.8g; Carbohydrate 77.6g, of which sugars 5.6g; Fat 9g, of which saturates 3.8g; Cholesterol 14mg; Calcium 128mg; Fibre 2.9g; Sodium 97mg.

RED PEPPER RISOTTO ★★

THIS PEPPER-BASED RISOTTO MAKES A SATISFYING AND DELICIOUS MEAL. IT IS IDEAL SERVED WITH A MIXED BABY LEAF SALAD AND FRESHLY BAKED ITALIAN BREAD.

SERVES FOUR

INGREDIENTS

    3 large red (bell) peppers
    15ml/1 tbsp olive oil
    3 large garlic cloves, thinly sliced
    400g/14oz can chopped tomatoes
    225g/8oz can chopped tomatoes
    2 bay leaves
    about 1.2–1.5 litres/2–2½ pints/
      5–6¼ cups vegetable stock
    450g/1lb/2¼ cups arborio rice or
      long grain brown rice
    6 fresh basil leaves, shredded
    salt and ground black pepper

1 Preheat the grill (broiler) to high. Put the peppers in the grill pan and cook until the skins are blackened and blistered all over. Transfer the peppers to a bowl, cover with a clean, damp dish towel and leave for 10 minutes. Peel off and discard the skins, then slice the peppers, discarding the cores and seeds. Set aside.

2 Heat the oil in a wide, shallow, non-stick pan. Add the garlic and tomatoes and cook gently for 5 minutes, stirring occasionally, then add the prepared pepper slices and the bay leaves. Stir well, then cook gently for 15 minutes, stirring occasionally.

3 Pour the vegetable stock into a separate heavy pan and heat it to simmering point. Stir the rice into the vegetable mixture and cook for about 2 minutes, then add two or three ladlefuls of the hot stock. Cook until all the stock has been absorbed into the rice, stirring occasionally.

VARIATION
Use yellow or green (bell) peppers or mixed (bell) peppers in place of all red.

4 Continue to add stock, making sure each addition has been absorbed before adding the next. When the rice is cooked and tender, season to taste.

5 Remove the pan from the heat, cover and leave to stand for 10 minutes. Remove and discard the bay leaves, then stir in the shredded basil. Serve.

Energy 501Kcal/2098kJ; Protein 10.9g; Carbohydrate 103.8g, of which sugars 13.6g; Fat 4.4g, of which saturates 0.7g; Cholesterol 0mg; Calcium 44mg; Fibre 3.9g; Sodium 20mg.

RISOTTO <u>WITH</u> BASIL <u>AND</u> RICOTTA ★★

THIS IS A WELL-FLAVOURED, LIGHT VEGETARIAN RISOTTO, WHICH BENEFITS FROM THE DISTINCTIVE PUNGENCY OF BASIL, MELLOWED WITH SMOOTH RICOTTA.

SERVES FOUR

INGREDIENTS
   10ml/2 tsp olive oil
   1 onion, finely chopped
   275g/10oz/scant 1½ cups risotto rice
   1 litre/1¾ pints/4 cups simmering
      vegetable stock
   175g/6oz/¾ cup ricotta cheese
   50g/2oz/generous 1 cup finely
      chopped fresh basil leaves, plus
      extra leaves to garnish
   40g/1½oz/½ cup freshly grated
      Parmesan cheese
   salt and ground black pepper

1 Heat the oil in a large, non-stick pan and cook the onion pieces over a gentle heat stirring frequently until they are soft.

2 Stir in the rice. Cook for a few minutes until the rice is coated with oil and is slightly translucent, stirring.

3 Pour in about a quarter of the stock. Cook until all the stock has been absorbed, stirring, then add another ladleful of stock. Continue in this manner, adding more stock when the previous ladleful has been absorbed, for about 20 minutes, or until the rice is just tender.

4 Spoon the ricotta cheese into a bowl and break it up a little with a fork. Stir into the risotto along with the basil and Parmesan. Adjust the seasoning to taste, then cover and allow to stand for 2–3 minutes before serving, garnished with basil leaves.

Energy 373Kcal/1557kJ; Protein 16.1g; Carbohydrate 57.9g, of which sugars 2.7g; Fat 8.8g, of which saturates 4.6g; Cholesterol 21mg; Calcium 213mg; Fibre 0.8g; Sodium 305mg.

ROSEMARY RISOTTO <u>WITH</u> BORLOTTI BEANS ★★

THIS IS A TASTY, LOW-FAT RISOTTO WITH A SUBTLE AND COMPLEX TASTE, FROM THE HEADY FLAVOURS OF ROSEMARY TO THE SAVOURY BEANS AND THE RICH TASTES OF THE CHEESES.

SERVES FOUR

INGREDIENTS
   400g/14oz can borlotti beans
   10ml/2 tsp olive oil
   1 onion, chopped
   2 garlic cloves, crushed
   275g/10oz/scant 1½ cups risotto rice
   175ml/6fl oz/¾ cup dry white wine
   900ml–1 litre/1½–1¾ pints/
      3¾–4 cups simmering
      vegetable stock
   30ml/2 tbsp mascarpone
   40g/1½oz/½ cup freshly grated
      Parmesan cheese, plus extra
      to serve (optional)
   5ml/1 tsp chopped fresh rosemary
   salt and ground black pepper

1 Drain the canned borlotti beans, rinse them well under plenty of cold water and drain again.

2 Purée about two-thirds of the beans fairly coarsely in a blender or food processor. Set the remainder aside.

3 Heat the oil in a large, non-stick pan and gently cook the onion and garlic for 6–8 minutes, or until very soft. Add the rice and cook over a medium heat for a few minutes until the grains are thoroughly coated in oil and are slightly translucent, stirring constantly.

VARIATION
Fresh thyme or marjoram could be used for this risotto instead of rosemary, if you prefer. Experiment with different herbs to make your own speciality dish.

4 Pour in the wine. Cook over a medium heat for 2–3 minutes until the wine has been absorbed, stirring constantly. Gradually add the stock, a ladleful at a time, waiting for each quantity to be absorbed before adding more, and stirring constantly.

5 When the rice is about three-quarters cooked, stir in the bean purée. Continue to cook the risotto, adding any stock that remains, until it has reached a creamy consistency and the rice is tender but still has a bit of "bite".

6 Add the reserved beans, with the mascarpone, Parmesan and rosemary, then season to taste with salt and pepper. Stir thoroughly, then cover and leave to stand for about 5 minutes, so that the risotto absorbs the flavours fully and the rice finishes cooking. Serve with extra Parmesan, if you like.

Energy 419Kcal/1752kJ; Protein 15.1g; Carbohydrate 68.8g, of which sugars 3.9g; Fat 6.2g, of which saturates 2.7g; Cholesterol 12mg; Calcium 198mg; Fibre 4.5g; Sodium 412mg.

BARLEY RISOTTO WITH SQUASH AND LEEKS ★★

THIS IS MORE LIKE A SEASONED RICE PILAFF THAN A CLASSIC RISOTTO. LEEKS, ROASTED BUTTERNUT SQUASH OR ANOTHER WINTER SQUASH GO REALLY WELL TOGETHER WITH THIS EARTHY GRAIN.

SERVES SIX

INGREDIENTS

200g/7oz/1 cup pearl barley
1 butternut squash, peeled, seeded and cut into chunks
10ml/2 tsp chopped fresh thyme
30ml/2 tbsp olive oil
15g/½oz/1 tbsp butter
4 leeks, cut into fairly thick diagonal slices
2 garlic cloves, finely chopped
175g/6oz/2¼ cups chestnut mushrooms, sliced
2 carrots, coarsely grated
about 120ml/4fl oz/½ cup vegetable stock
30ml/2 tbsp chopped fresh flat leaf parsley
25g/1oz/⅓ cup fresh Parmesan cheese, grated or shaved
45ml/3 tbsp pumpkin seeds, toasted, or chopped walnuts
salt and ground black pepper

1 Rinse the pearl barley, then cook it in a pan of simmering water, keeping the pan part-covered, for 35–45 minutes, or until tender. Drain. Preheat the oven to 200°C/400°F/Gas 6.

2 Place the squash in a roasting pan with half the thyme. Season with pepper and toss with half the oil. Roast in the oven for 30–35 minutes, until the squash is tender and beginning to brown, stirring once.

3 Heat half the butter with the remaining olive oil in a large non-stick frying pan. Add the leeks and garlic and cook gently for 5 minutes. Add the mushrooms and remaining thyme, then cook until the liquid from the mushrooms evaporates and they begin to fry.

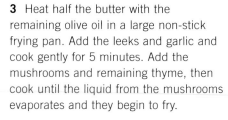

4 Stir in the carrots and cook for about 2 minutes, then add the pearl barley and most of the vegetable stock. Season well and partially cover the pan. Cook for a further 5 minutes. Pour in the remaining stock if the mixture seems dry.

5 Stir in the parsley, the remaining butter and half the cheese, then stir in the squash. Adjust the seasoning to taste and serve immediately, sprinkled with the toasted pumpkin seeds or walnuts and the remaining cheese.

COOK'S TIP
To chop fresh parsley quickly and easily, remove the stems and wash and dry the sprigs. Place the parsley sprigs in a jug or cup and snip the parsley into small pieces inside the jug or cup, using a pair of kitchen scissors.

VARIATIONS
• Make the risotto with brown rice instead of the pearl barley – cook following the packet instructions and continue from Step 2.
• Any type of mushrooms can be used in this recipe – try sliced field (portabello) mushrooms for a hearty flavour.

Energy 237Kcal/1000kJ; Protein 7.3g; Carbohydrate 34.8g, of which sugars 5.5g; Fat 8.6g, of which saturates 3g; Cholesterol 10mg; Calcium 121mg; Fibre 4.1g; Sodium 69mg.

SPICED VEGETABLE COUSCOUS ★★

THIS TASTY LOW-FAT VEGETARIAN MAIN COURSE IS EASY TO MAKE AND CAN BE PREPARED WITH ANY NUMBER OF SEASONAL VEGETABLES SUCH AS SPINACH, PEAS, BROAD BEANS OR CORN.

SERVES SIX

INGREDIENTS
    25ml/5 tsp olive oil
    1 large onion, finely chopped
    2 garlic cloves, crushed
    15ml/1 tbsp tomato purée (paste)
    2.5ml/½ tsp ground turmeric
    2.5ml/½ tsp cayenne pepper
    5ml/1 tsp ground coriander
    5ml/1 tsp ground cumin
    225g/8oz cauliflower florets
    225g/8oz baby carrots, trimmed
    1 red (bell) pepper, seeded and diced
    225g/8oz courgettes (zucchini),
        sliced
    400g/14oz can chickpeas, rinsed
        and drained
    4 beefsteak tomatoes, skinned
        and sliced
    45ml/3 tbsp chopped fresh
        coriander (cilantro)
    salt and ground black pepper
    fresh coriander sprigs, to garnish
For the couscous
    2.5ml/½ tsp salt
    450g/1lb/2⅔ cups couscous
    25g/1oz/2 tbsp butter or
        30ml/2 tbsp sunflower oil

1 Heat 15ml/1 tbsp olive oil in a large non-stick pan, add the onion and garlic and cook until soft and translucent. Stir in the tomato purée, turmeric, cayenne, ground coriander and cumin. Cook for 2 minutes, stirring.

2 Add the cauliflower, baby carrots and red pepper, with enough water to come halfway up the vegetables. Bring to the boil, then reduce the heat, cover and simmer for 10 minutes.

3 Add the courgettes, chickpeas and tomatoes to the pan and cook for 10 minutes. Stir in the fresh coriander and seasoning. Keep hot.

4 To cook the couscous, bring about 475ml/16fl oz/2 cups water to the boil in a large pan. Add the remaining olive oil and the salt. Remove the pan from the heat and add the couscous, stirring. Allow to swell for 2 minutes.

5 Add the butter or sunflower oil, and heat through gently, stirring to separate the grains.

6 Turn the couscous out on to a warm serving dish, and spoon the cooked vegetables on top, pouring over any liquid. Garnish with coriander sprigs and serve immediately.

Energy 382Kcal/1597kJ; Protein 13.3g; Carbohydrate 63g, of which sugars 12.4g; Fat 10g, of which saturates 1.3g; Cholesterol 0mg; Calcium 108mg; Fibre 7.1g; Sodium 187mg.

SPICY CHICKPEA AND AUBERGINE STEW ★★

SPICES ARE ESPECIALLY TYPICAL OF DISHES FROM THE NORTH OF GREECE, ALTHOUGH AUBERGINES AND CHICKPEAS ARE ENJOYED ALL OVER THE COUNTRY. THIS IS A HEARTY AND AROMATIC STEW.

SERVES FOUR

INGREDIENTS
    3 large aubergines (eggplants), diced
    200g/7oz/generous 1 cup dried
      chickpeas, soaked overnight
      in cold water
    25ml/5 tsp olive oil
    3 garlic cloves, finely chopped
    2 large onions, chopped
    2.5ml/½ tsp ground cumin
    2.5ml/½ tsp ground cinnamon
    2.5ml/½ tsp ground coriander
    3 x 400g/14oz cans chopped
      tomatoes
    salt and ground black pepper
    hot cooked rice, to serve
For the garnish
    10ml/2 tsp extra virgin olive oil
    1 onion, sliced
    1 garlic clove, sliced
    a few sprigs of fresh coriander
      (cilantro)

1 Place the diced aubergines in a colander and sprinkle them with plenty of salt. Sit the colander in a bowl and leave for at least 30 minutes, to allow the bitter juices to escape. Rinse thoroughly with cold water and pat dry on kitchen paper. Set aside.

2 Drain the chickpeas and put them in a large pan with enough water to cover them. Bring to the boil over a medium heat, then reduce the heat and simmer for 30 minutes, or until tender. Drain them thoroughly. Set aside.

3 Heat the oil in a large, non-stick pan. Add the garlic and onions and cook gently until soft. Add the ground spices and cook for a few seconds, stirring. Add the diced aubergine and stir to coat with the spices and onions. Cook for 5 minutes. Add the tomatoes, chickpeas and seasoning. Cover and simmer for 20 minutes.

4 To make the garnish, heat the olive oil in a non-stick frying pan and, when very hot, add the sliced onion and garlic. Fry until golden and crisp.

5 Serve the thick stew with cooked rice, topped with the crispy fried onion and garlic, and garnished with sprigs of fresh coriander.

Energy 303Kcal/1281kJ; Protein 15.3g; Carbohydrate 45.3g, of which sugars 19.2g; Fat 8.2g, of which saturates 1.2g; Cholesterol 0mg; Calcium 141mg; Fibre 12.8g; Sodium 53mg.

AROMATIC CHICKPEA AND SPINACH CURRY ★★

HIGH IN FIBRE, THIS HEARTY, WARMING LOW-FAT CURRY TASTES GREAT AND BOOSTS VITALITY WITH ESSENTIAL VITAMINS. SERVE IT WITH SPICY MANGO CHUTNEY COMBINED WITH COOLING MINT RAITA.

SERVES FOUR

INGREDIENTS

- 15ml/1 tbsp sunflower oil
- 1 large onion, finely chopped
- 2 garlic cloves, crushed
- 2.5cm/1in piece of fresh root ginger, finely chopped
- 1 fresh green chilli, seeded and finely chopped
- 30ml/2 tbsp medium curry paste
- 10ml/2 tsp ground cumin
- 5ml/1 tsp ground turmeric
- 225g/8oz can chopped tomatoes
- 1 green or red (bell) pepper, seeded and chopped
- 300ml/½ pint/1¼ cups vegetable stock
- 15ml/1 tbsp tomato purée (paste)
- 450g/1lb fresh spinach
- 425g/15oz can chickpeas, rinsed and drained
- 45ml/3 tbsp chopped fresh coriander (cilantro)
- 5ml/1 tsp garam masala (optional)
- salt

1 Heat the oil in a large, heavy, non-stick pan and cook the onion, garlic, ginger and chilli over a gentle heat for about 5 minutes, or until the onion has softened, but not browned. Stir in the curry paste, mix thoroughly and cook for a further minute, then stir in the ground cumin and turmeric. Stir over a low heat for a further minute.

2 Add the tomatoes and pepper and stir to coat with the spice mixture. Pour in the stock, then stir in the tomato purée. Bring to the boil, reduce the heat, cover and simmer for 15 minutes.

3 Remove any coarse stalks from the spinach, then rinse the leaves thoroughly, drain them and tear into large pieces. Add them to the pan, in batches, adding a handful more as each batch cooks down and wilts.

4 Stir in the chickpeas, cover and cook gently for a further 5 minutes. Add the chopped coriander, season to taste with salt and stir well. Spoon into a warmed serving bowl and sprinkle with the garam masala, if using. Serve immediately.

VARIATION
Use 4–6 shallots in place of the onion.

Energy 239Kcal/1000kJ; Protein 12.9g; Carbohydrate 32.7g, of which sugars 13.9g; Fat 7.2g, of which saturates 0.9g; Cholesterol 0mg; Calcium 274mg; Fibre 9.5g; Sodium 397mg.

BALTI STIR-FRIED VEGETABLES WITH CASHEWS ★★

THIS VERSATILE STIR-FRY RECIPE WILL ACCOMMODATE MOST COMBINATIONS OF VEGETABLES SO FEEL FREE TO EXPERIMENT. THE CASHEW NUTS ADD A DELICIOUS TEXTURE AND INTEREST.

SERVES FOUR

INGREDIENTS
  2 carrots
  1 red (bell) pepper, seeded
  1 green (bell) pepper, seeded
  2 courgettes (zucchini)
  115g/4oz green beans, halved
  a bunch of spring onions (scallions)
  15ml/1 tbsp extra virgin olive oil
  4–6 curry leaves
  2.5ml/½ tsp cumin seeds
  4 dried red chillies
  10–12 cashew nuts
  5ml/1 tsp salt
  30ml/2 tbsp lemon juice
  fresh mint leaves, to garnish

1 Cut the carrots, peppers and courgettes into matchsticks, halve the beans and chop the spring onions. Set aside.

2 Heat the oil in a non-stick frying pan or wok and stir-fry the curry leaves, cumin seeds and dried chillies for 1 minute.

COOK'S TIP
When making stir-fries, it is a good idea to use a non-stick wok (or frying pan) to minimize the amount of oil needed. However, it cannot be heated to the same high temperature as a conventional wok.

3 Add the prepared vegetables and nuts and toss them over the heat for 3–4 minutes. Add the salt and lemon juice and stir-fry for a further 2 minutes, until the vegetables are tender-crisp.

4 Transfer to a warm dish and serve garnished with mint leaves. Serve with cooked brown or white rice or warm naan bread.

Energy 105Kcal/436kJ; Protein 4.2g; Carbohydrate 11.2g, of which sugars 10.1g; Fat 5.1g, of which saturates 0.9g; Cholesterol 0mg; Calcium 56mg; Fibre 3.9g; Sodium 510mg.

CREAMY LEMON PUY LENTILS ★★

THE COMBINATION OF LENTILS, SPRING ONIONS, TOMATO, LEMON, PEPPER AND CRÈME FRAÎCHE MAKES FOR A TANGY MEDITERRANEAN DISH. THE LENTILS PROVIDE A SLIGHTLY EARTHY FLAVOUR.

SERVES SIX

INGREDIENTS

    250g/9oz/generous 1 cup Puy lentils
    1 bay leaf
    15ml/1 tbsp olive oil
    4 spring onions (scallions), sliced
    2 large garlic cloves, chopped
    15ml/1 tbsp Dijon mustard
    finely grated rind and juice of
      1 large lemon
    4 plum tomatoes, seeded and diced
    6 eggs
    60ml/4 tbsp reduced-fat
      crème fraîche
    salt and ground black pepper
    30ml/2 tbsp chopped fresh flat leaf
      parsley, to garnish

1 Put the Puy lentils and bay leaf in a large pan, cover with cold water, and slowly bring to the boil. Reduce the heat and simmer, partially covered, for about 25 minutes, or until the lentils are tender. Stir the lentils occasionally and add more water, if necessary. Drain.

2 Heat the oil in a non-stick frying pan and cook the spring onions and garlic for about 1 minute or until softened. Add the Dijon mustard and lemon rind and juice and stir to mix.

COOK'S TIP
Puy lentils are the most prized of all lentils and they originate from Puy in France. They are tiny grey-green lentils, with a distinctive flavour. Unlike some lentils, they keep their shape and colour when cooked.

3 Stir the tomatoes and seasoning into the lentils with the onion mixture, then cook gently for 1–2 minutes until the tomatoes are heated through, but still retain their shape. Add a little water if the mixture becomes too dry.

4 Meanwhile, poach the eggs in a separate pan of lightly salted barely simmering water for 4 minutes, adding them one at a time. Place the lentil mixture on to six plates, and serve immediately with a poached egg on top.

Energy 244Kcal/1026kJ; Protein 17.3g; Carbohydrate 23.2g, of which sugars 3.1g; Fat 9.9g, of which saturates 3g; Cholesterol 190mg; Calcium 75mg; Fibre 4.5g; Sodium 85mg.

DESSERTS AND CAKES

Even though you may be watching your calorie and fat intake, this doesn't mean you have to miss out on enticing desserts and cakes. They round off many meals perfectly and the recipes that follow are both delicous and low in fat. Choose from delights such as Caribbean Baked Bananas, Filo-topped Apple Pie, Blackberry Charlotte, and Angel Cake.

TROPICAL COCONUT SORBET ★

DELICIOUSLY REFRESHING AND COOLING, THIS LOW-FAT TROPICAL SORBET CAN BE FOUND IN DIFFERENT VERSIONS ALL OVER SOUTH-EAST ASIA.

SERVES SIX

INGREDIENTS

175g/6oz/scant 1 cup caster
(superfine) sugar
120ml/4fl oz/½ cup coconut milk
50g/2oz/⅔ cup grated or desiccated
(dry unsweetened shredded) coconut
a squeeze of fresh lime juice
fresh mint leaves, to decorate

1 Place the sugar in a heavy pan and add 200ml/7fl oz/scant 1 cup water. Bring to the boil, stirring constantly until the sugar has dissolved completely. Reduce the heat and simmer for 5 minutes to make a light syrup.

2 Stir the coconut milk into the syrup, along with most of the coconut and the lime juice. Pour the mixture into a shallow bowl or freezer container and freeze for 1 hour.

3 Take the sorbet out of the freezer and beat it, or process it in a blender or food processor, until smooth and creamy, then return it to the freezer and leave until frozen.

4 Before serving, allow the sorbet to stand at room temperature for 10–15 minutes to soften slightly. Serve in small bowls and decorate with the remaining coconut and the mint leaves.

COOK'S TIP
Desiccated (dry unsweetened shredded) coconut is the shredded white flesh of fresh coconut from which all the moisture has been extracted. It is available either flaked or in fine or medium shredded strands. Desiccated coconut is suitable for both sweet and savoury dishes.

Energy 196Kcal/834kJ; Protein 1.1g; Carbohydrate 40.1g, of which sugars 40.1g; Fat 4.7g, of which saturates 3.9g; Cholesterol 0mg; Calcium 71mg; Fibre 0.9g; Sodium 209mg.

LEMON SORBET ★

*EATING THIS SMOOTH, TANGY, COMPLETELY FAT-FREE SORBET, PROVIDES A REFRESHING CHANGE OF TASTE
TO THE PALATE AFTER A MORE SPICY OR FULL-BODIED MAIN MEAL.*

SERVES SIX

INGREDIENTS
    200g/7oz/1 cup caster
      (superfine) sugar
    300ml/½ pint/1¼ cups water
    4 lemons, washed
    1 large (US extra large) egg white
    a little granulated sugar,
      for sprinkling

1 Put the caster sugar and water into a heavy pan and bring slowly to the boil, stirring occasionally until the sugar has just dissolved.

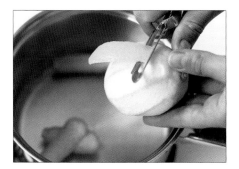

2 Using a swivel vegetable peeler, thinly pare the rind from two of the lemons directly into the pan. Simmer for about 2 minutes without stirring, then remove the pan from the heat. Leave the syrup to cool, then chill.

3 Squeeze the juice from all the lemons and carefully strain it into the syrup, making sure all the pips are removed. Take the lemon rind out of the syrup and set it aside until you make the decoration.

4 If you have an ice cream maker, strain the syrup into the machine tub and churn for 10 minutes until it thickens.

5 Lightly whisk the egg white with a fork and pour it into the machine. Continue to churn for 10–15 minutes, until firm enough to scoop.

6 Working by hand, strain the syrup into a plastic tub or a similar shallow freezerproof container and freeze for 4 hours, until the mixture is mushy.

7 Scoop the mushy mixture into a food processor and process until smooth. Lightly whisk the egg white with a fork until it is just frothy. Spoon the sorbet back into its container and beat in the egg white. Return to the freezer for 1 hour.

8 To make the sugared rind decoration, use the blanched rind from Step 2. Cut it into very thin strips and sprinkle with granulated sugar on a plate. Scoop the sorbet into bowls or glasses and decorate with sugared lemon rind.

VARIATION
Sorbet can be made from any citrus fruit. As a guide, you will need 300ml/½ pint/ 1¼ cups of fresh fruit juice and the pared rind of half the squeezed fruits. For example, use four oranges or two oranges and two lemons, or, to make a grapefruit sorbet, use the rind of one ruby grapefruit and the juice of two.

Energy 135Kcal/574kJ; Protein 0.7g; Carbohydrate 35.1g, of which sugars 35.1g; Fat 0g, of which saturates 0g; Cholesterol 0mg; Calcium 19mg; Fibre 0g; Sodium 12mg.

FRESH FRUIT SALAD ★

ORANGES ARE AN ESSENTIAL INGREDIENT FOR A DELICIOUS AND REFRESHING LIGHT FRUIT SALAD, WHICH CAN INCLUDE ANY FRUIT IN SEASON. STRAWBERRIES, PEACHES AND APPLES ENTICE THE TASTE BUDS.

SERVES SIX

INGREDIENTS
    2 eating apples
    2 oranges
    2 peaches
    16–20 strawberries
    30ml/2 tbsp lemon juice
    15–30ml/1–2 tbsp orange
      flower water
    icing (confectioners') sugar,
      to taste (optional)
    a few sprigs of fresh mint,
      to decorate

COOK'S TIP
There are no rules with this fruit salad, and you could use almost any fruit that you like. Oranges, however, should form the base and apples give a delightful contrast in texture.

1 Peel and core the apples and cut into thin slices. Cut a thin slice of peel and pith from both ends of the oranges, then cut off the remaining peel and pith. Cut out each segment leaving the membrane behind. Squeeze the juice from the membrane and retain.

2 Blanch the peaches in a pan of boiling water for 1 minute. Peel off the skin and cut the flesh into thick slices.

3 Hull the strawberries, if you like, and halve or quarter them if large. Place all the prepared fruit in a large serving bowl.

4 Mix together the lemon juice, orange flower water and any orange juice. Taste and add a little icing sugar to sweeten, if you like. Pour the fruit juice mixture over the salad and serve decorated with mint leaves.

Energy 47Kcal/202kJ; Protein 1.2g; Carbohydrate 11g, of which sugars 11g; Fat 0.1g, of which saturates 0g; Cholesterol 0mg; Calcium 32mg; Fibre 2.1g; Sodium 5mg.

DRIED FRUIT SALAD ★

A WONDERFUL COMBINATION OF FRESH AND DRIED FRUIT FLAVOURED WITH HONEY AND LEMON, THIS MAKES AN EXCELLENT LOW-FAT DESSERT. YOU CAN SUBSTITUTE FROZEN RASPBERRIES OR BLACKBERRIES.

SERVES FOUR

INGREDIENTS
    115g/4oz/½ cup dried apricots
    115g/4oz/½ cup dried peaches
    1 eating pear
    1 eating apple
    1 orange
    115g/4oz/⅔ cup mixed raspberries
      and blackberries
    1 cinnamon stick
    50g/2oz/¼ cup caster
      (superfine) sugar
    15ml/1 tbsp clear honey
    30ml/2 tbsp lemon juice

1 Place the apricots and peaches in a bowl and add water to cover. Set aside to soak for 1–2 hours until plump, then drain well and halve or quarter the fruit.

2 Peel and core the pear and apple, then dice the flesh. Cut a thin slice of peel and pith from each end of the orange, then cut off the remaining peel and pith. Cut the orange into wedges. Place all the prepared fruit in a large pan with the raspberries and blackberries.

3 Add 600ml/1 pint/2½ cups water, the cinnamon stick, sugar and honey, and bring to the boil. Cover and simmer gently for about 10 minutes, then remove the pan from the heat. Stir in the lemon juice. Leave to cool completely, then transfer the fruit and syrup to a bowl and chill for 1–2 hours before serving.

Energy 185Kcal/790kJ; Protein 2.9g; Carbohydrate 45.3g, of which sugars 45.3g; Fat 0.5g, of which saturates 0g; Cholesterol 0mg; Calcium 64mg; Fibre 5.8g; Sodium 12mg.

CARIBBEAN BAKED BANANAS ★

TENDER BAKED BANANAS IN A RICH AND SPICY SAUCE OF GROUND ALLSPICE AND GINGER CREATES THIS DELICIOUS LOW-FAT DESSERT, IDEAL FOR THOSE WITH A SWEET TOOTH.

SERVES FOUR

INGREDIENTS

30ml/2 tbsp reduced-fat spread
8 firm ripe bananas
juice of 1 lime
75g/3oz/scant ½ cup soft dark
  brown sugar
5ml/1 tsp ground allspice
2.5ml/½ tsp ground ginger
seeds from 6 cardamom pods crushed
30ml/2 tbsp rum
pared lime rind, to decorate
half-fat crème fraîche, to serve
  (optional)

1 Preheat the oven to 200°C/400°F/ Gas 6. Use a little of the reduced-fat spread to grease a shallow baking dish large enough to hold the bananas snugly in a single layer.

COOK'S TIPS

Choose firm, ripe bananas for this dessert, but avoid very ripe bananas with brown speckled skins as these may be slightly too ripe and soft for this recipe. Use a stainless steel knife to cut the bananas, to help prevent them browning or discolouring, before you add the spicy topping.

2 Peel the bananas and cut them in half lengthways. Arrange the bananas in the dish and pour over the lime juice.

3 Mix the sugar, allspice, ginger and crushed cardamom seeds in a bowl. Scatter the mixture over the bananas. Dot with the remaining reduced-fat spread. Bake in the oven for 15 minutes, or until the bananas are soft, basting once.

4 Remove the dish from the oven. Warm the rum in a small pan or metal soup ladle, pour it over the bananas and set it alight.

5 As soon as the flames die down, decorate the dessert with the pared lime rind. Serve while still hot and add a small dollop of reduced-fat crème fraîche to each portion, if you like.

VARIATION

For a version that will appeal more to children, use orange juice instead of lime and leave out the rum.

Energy 253Kcal/1069kJ; Protein 2.2g; Carbohydrate 52.1g, of which sugars 48.9g; Fat 3.5g, of which saturates 1g; Cholesterol 0mg; Calcium 21mg; Fibre 1.6g; Sodium 51mg.

FILO-TOPPED APPLE PIE ★

WITH ITS SCRUNCHY FILO TOPPING AND ONLY A SMALL AMOUNT OF REDUCED-FAT SPREAD, THIS RECIPE CREATES A REALLY LIGHT AND HEALTHY DESSERT.

SERVES SIX

INGREDIENTS
  900g/2lb Bramley or other
    cooking apples
  75g/3oz/6 tbsp caster
    (superfine) sugar
  finely grated rind of 1 lemon
  15ml/1 tbsp lemon juice
  75g/3oz/generous ½ cup sultanas
    (golden raisins)
  2.5ml/½ tsp ground cinnamon
  4 large sheets filo pastry, thawed
    if frozen
  30ml/2 tbsp reduced-fat
    spread, melted
  icing (confectioners') sugar,
    for dusting

1 Peel, core and dice the apples. Place them in a pan with the caster sugar and lemon rind. Drizzle the lemon juice over. Bring to the boil, stir well, then cook for 5 minutes or until the apples soften.

2 Stir in the sultanas and cinnamon. Spoon the mixture into a 1.2 litre/2 pint/ 5 cup pie dish and level the top. Leave to cool.

COOK'S TIP
Filo pastry is available frozen or as chilled fresh pastry in sheets of varying sizes. Thaw frozen filo thoroughly (according to the instructions on the packet) and let both defrosted and chilled fresh filo pastry come to room temperature in its box before you use it.

3 Preheat the oven to 180°C/350°F/ Gas 4. Place a pie funnel in the centre of the fruit. Brush each sheet of filo pastry with melted reduced-fat spread. Scrunch up the pastry loosely and place on the fruit to cover it completely.

4 Bake in the oven for 20–30 minutes or until the filo is golden. Dust the pie with sifted icing sugar before serving.

VARIATIONS
• To make filo crackers, cut the greased filo into 20cm/8in wide strips. Spoon a little of the filling along one end of each strip, leaving the sides clear. Roll up and twist the ends to make a cracker. Brush with a little more melted reduced-fat spread, and bake in the oven for 20 minutes.
• Use raisins or chopped ready-to-eat dried apricots in place of sultanas (golden raisins). Use ground mixed spice or ginger in place of ground cinnamon.

Energy 198Kcal/843kJ; Protein 2.2g; Carbohydrate 44.8g, of which sugars 35.3g; Fat 2.4g, of which saturates 0.6g; Cholesterol 0mg; Calcium 38mg; Fibre 3g; Sodium 44mg.

SUMMER BERRY CRÊPES ★

LIGHT AND DELICIOUS CRÊPES MAKE A PERFECT FLUFFY 'ENVELOPE' FOR THIS MIXTURE OF TANGY BERRY FRUITS. ADDING AND FLAMBÉING A LIQUEUR TAKES IT INTO ANOTHER DESSERT DIMENSION.

SERVES FOUR

INGREDIENTS

115g/4oz/1 cup self-raising
   (self-rising) flour
1 large (US extra large) egg
300ml/½ pint/1¼ cups
   skimmed milk
a few drops of pure vanilla extract
spray oil, for greasing
icing (confectioners') sugar,
   for dusting
For the fruit
15ml/1 tbsp reduced-fat spread
50g/2oz/¼ cup caster
   (superfine) sugar
juice of 2 oranges
thinly pared rind of ½ orange
350g/12oz/3 cups mixed summer
   berries, such as sliced strawberries,
   yellow or red raspberries,
   blueberries and redcurrants
45ml/3 tbsp Grand Marnier or other
   orange-flavoured liqueur

1 Preheat the oven to 150°C/300°F/ Gas 2. To make the crêpes, sift the flour into a large bowl and make a well in the centre. Break in the egg, then gradually whisk in the milk to make a smooth, creamy batter. Stir in the vanilla extract. Set the batter aside in a cool place for up to 30 minutes.

VARIATIONS

• Use self-raising (self-rising) wholemeal (whole-wheat) flour in place of white flour.
• Use soft light brown sugar in place of caster (superfine) sugar.

2 Apply a light, even coat of spray oil to an 18cm/7in non-stick frying pan. Whisk the batter, then pour a little of it into the hot pan, swirling to cover the base of the pan evenly. Cook until the mixture comes away from the sides and the crêpe is golden underneath.

3 Flip the crêpe over with a large palette knife or metal spatula and cook the other side briefly until it appears golden. Slide the crêpe on to a heatproof plate.

4 Make seven or so more crêpes in the same way, layering the crêpes one on top of the other, with sheets of baking parchment in between each one. Cover the crêpes with foil or another oven-proof plate and keep them hot in a warm oven.

5 To prepare the fruit, melt the reduced-fat spread in a heavy non-stick frying pan over a gentle heat, then stir in the caster sugar and cook gently. Add the orange juice and pared rind and cook until syrupy. Add the fruits and warm through (reserving some for decoration), then add the liqueur and set it alight. Shake the pan until the flames die down.

6 Fold the pancakes into quarters and arrange two on each serving plate. Spoon over the fruit mixture and dust with sifted icing sugar. Serve the remaining fruit separately in a serving bowl.

COOK'S TIPS

• Choose firm, ripe, plump summer berries that are uniform in colour and showing no signs of mould or rot. Choose berries such as strawberries with hulls or stalks intact (then remove them before use).
• For safety, when igniting a mixture for flambéing, use a long taper or long wooden match. Stand back as you set the mixture alight.

Energy 260Kcal/1099kJ; Protein 8g; Carbohydrate 45.9g, of which sugars 24.6g; Fat 3.5g, of which saturates 0.9g; Cholesterol 51mg; Calcium 235mg; Fibre 2.4g; Sodium 184mg.

AUTUMN PUDDING ★

SUMMER PUDDING IS FAR TOO GOOD TO BE RESERVED FOR THE SOFT FRUIT SEASON. HERE IS A DELICIOUS LOW-FAT AUTUMN VERSION, COMBINING APPLES, PLUMS AND BLACKBERRIES.

SERVES SIX

INGREDIENTS
  450g/1lb eating apples
  450g/1lb plums, halved and stoned
  225g/8oz/2 cups blackberries
  60ml/4 tbsp apple juice
  a little granulated sugar or honey,
    to sweeten (optional)
  8 slices wholemeal (whole-wheat)
    bread, crusts removed
  a fresh mint sprig and a blackberry,
    to decorate
  half-fat crème fraîche, to serve
    (optional)

VARIATIONS
Use white bread in place of wholemeal (whole-wheat) bread. Use autumn raspberries in place of blackberries.

1 Quarter the apples, peel and core them, then slice the apples into a pan. Add the plums, blackberries and apple juice. Cover and cook gently for 10–15 minutes until tender. Sweeten, if necessary, with a little sugar or honey, although the fruit should be sweet enough.

2 Line the bottom and sides of a 1.2 litre/2 pint/5 cup heatproof bowl with slices of bread, cut to fit. Press together tightly.

3 Spoon the fruit mixture into the bowl. Pour in just enough juice to moisten. Reserve any remaining juice.

4 Cover the fruit completely with the remaining bread. Fit a plate on top, so that it rests on the bread just below the rim. Stand the basin in a larger bowl to catch any juice. Place a weight on the plate and chill overnight.

5 Turn the pudding out on to a serving plate and pour the reserved juice over any areas that have not absorbed the juice. Decorate with the mint sprig and blackberry. Serve with a little crème fraîche, if you like.

Energy 153Kcal/654kJ; Protein 4.8g; Carbohydrate 33g, of which sugars 17.3g; Fat 1.4g, of which saturates 0.2g; Cholesterol 0mg; Calcium 71mg; Fibre 5.6g; Sodium 199mg.

BLACKBERRY CHARLOTTE ★

A CLASSIC LOW-FAT HOT, MOULDED FRUIT PUDDING, THE PERFECT REWARD FOR AN AFTERNOON'S BLACKBERRY PICKING. USE WHITE BREAD AND A LOW-FAT SPREAD INSTEAD OF BUTTER.

SERVES FOUR

INGREDIENTS
    30ml/2 tbsp reduced-fat spread
    175g/6oz/3 cups fresh white
      breadcrumbs
    50g/2oz/¼ cup soft light brown sugar
    60ml/4 tbsp golden (light corn) syrup
    finely grated rind and juice of
      2 lemons
    450g/1lb cooking apples
    450g/1lb/4 cups blackberries

1 Preheat the oven to 180°C/350°F/ Gas 4. Melt the reduced-fat spread in a non-stick pan with the breadcrumbs. Cook gently for 5–7 minutes, until the crumbs are golden and fairly crisp, stirring frequently. Remove the pan from the heat and leave to cool slightly.

2 Gently heat the sugar, syrup and lemon rind and juice in a separate small pan. Add the crumbs and mix well.

3 Cut the apples into quarters, then peel them and remove the cores. Slice the wedges thinly.

4 Arrange a thin layer of blackberries in an ovenproof baking dish. Top with a thin layer of crumbs, then a thin layer of apples, topping the fruit with another thin layer of crumbs. Repeat the process with another layer of blackberries, followed by a layer of crumbs, then apples.

5 Continue until you have used up all the ingredients, finishing with a layer of crumbs.

6 Bake in the oven for 30 minutes, or until the crumbs are golden and the fruit is soft. Serve immediately.

VARIATION
Use blueberries or raspberries in place of blackberries.

COOK'S TIP
When layering the fruit and crumbs, the mixture should be piled well above the top edge of the dish, because it shrinks during cooking.

Energy 346Kcal/1468kJ; Protein 7g; Carbohydrate 74.6g, of which sugars 41.8g; Fat 4.2g, of which saturates 0.9g; Cholesterol 0mg; Calcium 120mg; Fibre 6.3g; Sodium 427mg.

ANGEL CAKE ★

A DELICIOUS LIGHT CAKE TO SERVE AS A LOW-FAT DESSERT FOR A SPECIAL OCCASION.

SERVES TEN

INGREDIENTS

40g/1½oz/⅓ cup cornflour
   (cornstarch)
40g/1½oz/⅓ cup plain
   (all-purpose) flour
8 egg whites
225g/8oz/generous 1 cup caster
   (superfine) sugar, plus extra
   for sprinkling
5ml/1 tsp vanilla extract
90ml/6 tbsp orange-flavoured glacé
   icing, 4–6 physalis and a little icing
   (confectioners') sugar, to decorate

VARIATION

Use lemon-flavoured glacé icing,
if you prefer.

1 Preheat the oven to 180°C/350°F/
Gas 4. Sift both flours on to a sheet of
baking parchment. Set aside.

2 Whisk the egg whites in a clean, dry
large bowl until very stiff, then gradually
add the caster sugar and vanilla extract,
whisking until the mixture is thick
and glossy.

3 Gently fold in the flour mixture with a
large metal spoon. Spoon into an
ungreased 25cm/10in angel cake tin
and smooth the surface. Bake in the
oven for about 45–50 minutes, until the
cake springs back when lightly pressed
in the centre.

4 Sprinkle a piece of baking parchment
with caster sugar and set an egg cup in
the centre. Invert the cake tin over the
paper, balancing it carefully on the egg
cup. When cold, the cake will drop out
of the tin.

5 Transfer the cake to a serving
plate, spoon over the glacé icing,
spreading it evenly, arrange the physalis
on top and then dust with sifted icing
sugar. Serve in slices.

COOK'S TIP

If you prefer, omit the glacé icing and
physalis and simply dust the cake with a
little sifted icing (confectioners') sugar – it
is delicious to serve as a coffee-time treat,
and also makes the perfect accompaniment
to vanilla yogurt ice for a dessert.

Energy 126Kcal/536kJ; Protein 2.8g; Carbohydrate 30.3g, of which sugars 23.6g; Fat 0.1g, of which saturates 0g; Cholesterol 0mg; Calcium 19mg; Fibre 0.1g; Sodium 52mg.

CINNAMON APPLE GÂTEAU ★

APPLE AND CINNAMON ARE A TRIED AND TESTED COMBINATION TO GIVE YOU A MOREISH CAKE.

SERVES TWELVE

INGREDIENTS
  3 eggs
  115g/4oz/generous ½ cup caster
    (superfine) sugar
  75g/3oz/⅔ cup plain (all-purpose) flour
  5ml/1 tsp ground cinnamon
For the filling and topping
  4 large eating apples
  60ml/4 tbsp clear honey
  15ml/1 tbsp water
  75g/3oz/generous ½ cup sultanas
    (golden raisins)
  2.5ml/½ tsp ground cinnamon
  350g/12oz/1½ cups low-fat
    soft cheese
  60ml/4 tbsp low-fat plain fromage
    frais or low-fat soft cheese
  10ml/2 tsp lemon juice
  45ml/3 tbsp apricot glaze or apricot
    jam, heated until melted
  fresh mint sprigs, to decorate

1 Preheat the oven to 190°C/375°F/ Gas 5. Grease and line a 23cm/9in shallow round cake tin (pan). Place the eggs and caster sugar in a bowl and beat with a hand-held electric whisk until thick and mousse-like. (When the whisk is lifted, a trail should remain on the surface of the mixture for at least 15 seconds.)

2 Sift the flour and cinnamon over the egg mixture and fold in with a large metal spoon. Pour the mixture evenly into the prepared tin and bake in the oven for 25–30 minutes, or until the cake springs back when lightly pressed. Turn the cake on to a wire rack to cool.

3 To make the filling, peel, core and slice 3 of the apples and put them in a pan. Add 30ml/2 tbsp of the honey and the water. Cover and cook over a gentle heat for about 10 minutes. Remove the pan from the heat, add the sultanas and cinnamon, stir well, replace the lid and leave to cool.

4 Put the soft cheese in a bowl with the remaining honey, the fromage frais – or soft cheese if you prefer – and half the lemon juice. Beat until the mixture is smooth.

5 Halve the cake horizontally, place the bottom half on a chopping board and drizzle over any liquid from the apples. Spread with two-thirds of the cheese mixture, then top with the apple filling. Fit the top of the cake in place.

6 Swirl the remaining cheese mixture over the top of the sponge. Core and slice the remaining apple, sprinkle with the remaining lemon juice and use to decorate the edge of the cake. Brush the apple slices with the apricot glaze and decorate with mint sprigs.

Energy 166Kcal/704kJ; Protein 6.8g; Carbohydrate 29g, of which sugars 24.2g; Fat 3.9g, of which saturates 1.9g; Cholesterol 55mg; Calcium 60mg; Fibre 0.9g; Sodium 153mg.

INDEX